CONFESSIONS OF A SEASICK DOCTOR

Confessions of a Seasick Doctor

An account of life on a Mercy Ship

CHRISTINE ARONEY-SINE

YOUTH WITH A MISSION

MARC
Crowborough

British Library Cataloguing Data
A catalogue record for this book is available
from the British Library.

ISBN: 1 85424 295 4

Produced by Bookprint Creative Services
P.O. Box 827, BN21 3YJ, England for
MARC an imprint of Monarch Publications
Broadway House, The Broadway,
Crowborough, East Sussex, TN6 1HQ
Printed in Great Britain.

This book is dedicated to my good
friends Ruth Crow and Cheryl Mackey and
the thousands of other volunteers on ship and ashore
whose efforts helped bring the Mercy Ships
ministry into being

Contents

FOREWORD

I just recently had the opportunity of spending another day on board the *Anastasis*. She was visiting London for the third time, and I had the privilege of having several of my friends and their families on board for a tour. We went through the whole ship from bow to stern. They all marvelled at the size of the engines, the sense of power that one inevitably feels standing on the bridge, and then watched in amazement as the latest videos recounted the work done through this ministry. More than one of my guests concluded that they would just love to be part of the ministry of the *Anastasis*, at least for a while.

But what is it really like? What would it mean to live on board with hundreds of other people, regularly changing climates, nations and cultures as the ship moves from continent to continent? Dr Chris Aroney-Sine reveals the realities of life on board a Mercy Ship as skilfully as anyone to date. Realism and humour are interwoven on every page.

Dr Chris is thoroughly qualified to tell you about life on a Mercy Ship. She was numbered amongst the tiny handful of people who committed themselves to this ministry well before the first ship ever sailed. She then served, with increasing responsibilities, for many years, while the ministry developed and became increasingly effective.

These pages offer not just a glimpse, but real insights into the price that must be paid to do something significant with your life. They also reveal the joy and the pain of pioneering a significant ministry for the glory of God. Enjoy your reading – I did!

LYNN GREEN
Director for Europe,
Middle East and Africa,
Youth With A Mission

ACKNOWLEDGEMENTS

This book is not just the story of one person, nor does it reflect the work of a single author. I am indebted to the stories, input and critique of dozens of Mercy Ship volunteers past and present. I am also deeply grateful for all those who have supported me with their finances, prayers and encouragement during my years of involvement in Mercy Ships, particularly my long-term supporters, New Life Centre, Christchurch New Zealand, Moana Lua Gardens Missionary Church, Hawaii, Bill and Karen Hansill, Forrest and Betty Bright, Jim and Cecilia Leininger, Louise Berghouse, Andrew and Jeri Geleris, Beverley Willan, Ray and Irma de Zylva, Emil and Judith Nye, and Ray and Nettie Burge.

I would also like to thank Ruth Crow, Cheryl Mackey, Dr Gary Parker, Dave O'Connor, Patty Morehouse, Pam Courson, Becky Bynum, and Heather Choate who assisted me with valuable editorial advice. Of course I could not have completed this task without the support, encouragement and prayers of my husband, Tom Sine. Finally, I would like to thank Don Stephens, the President of Mercy Ships, who gave me the opportunity to be involved in the ministry of Mercy Ships around the world.

Chapter 1

HAVE BUCKET, WILL TRAVEL

I love the sea and the exhilaration of sailing. The waves crashing against the side of a ship, the wind whipping through my hair with the tantalizing smell of salt air wafting around me makes me feel energetically alive.

Unfortunately, whenever I sail, I get sick. Even sitting in a porch swing or lying in a hammock makes me ill and dizzy. So no one was more surprised than I was when I felt called to the *Anastasis*, a Christian Mercy Ship. It seemed improbable to me that I could ever become part of a seafaring mission. However God had different ideas.

Amazingly, I lived for almost twelve years on the *Anastasis*, and never adapted to the motion. Sometimes I endured weeks of continuous nausea and dizziness. However, it never restricted my activities as a doctor nor detracted from my sense of calling to this ministry. Let me share one small example from my rock and roll seafaring past.

As we sailed out of Olympia, Washington on the west coast of the US, I knew we were in for a bad blow. Ominous black clouds hung low over the grey, unfriendly sea and the dim twilight reflected off the angry white peaks already lapping hungrily at the ship's hull. The deck crew screwed my porthole shut, a sure sign that we were sailing into a serious storm. Everything aboard that could possibly move was battened down.

The hospital resembled the lost luggage department at the local railway station. Battered boxes containing our precious equipment nestled around the operating table. They were lined with blankets to protect their delicate contents then securely tied down. Wash sinks, cabinets, door hinges, and the operating table itself, in fact anything that was bolted to the walls, served as anchor points. Boxes of supplies, donated at the last minute, were tightly wedged together along the corridors. They would have to take their chances, there was nowhere else to put them. Ropes festooned the blanket-shrouded anaesthetic machines, patient trolleys and instrument tables like spiders' webs pinioning their prey.

The moment we began to roll, I took to my bed, praying fervently that I could stay there until we reached San Francisco. The ship twisted and turned helplessly as the gale force winds lashed the waves to a furious frenzy. Down, down, down we sank into the troughs that opened like the mouths of ravenous sea creatures beneath us. I fought desperately against the sensation that left my stomach separated from my body. Then we were hurled to the top of angry peaks that beckoned us with the full force of the Pacific Ocean behind them. That separated me from everything I had eaten in the past twenty-four hours.

Enormous waves thudded explosively against the hull, shooting streams of water high over the bow to crash against the vehicles and other machinery tied on the foredeck. Joints creaked and groaned in protest as the *Anastasis* rolled from twenty degrees on one side and over to an equally horrendous list on the other. At each impact we hovered motionless for a few seconds, then slid slowly forward down the steep slope to meet the next oncoming giant. The occasional resounding crash suggested that not everything on board was as tightly secured as it should have been.

By now, I was retching so badly I thought I would die. At times I was so miserable I wished I could. I staggered back to bed after one of my many trips to the toilet and watched in horror as the books in the bulkhead opposite me began to shift. The carpenter had assured me the slope of the wall was sufficient to keep them in place. Wrong! The ship gave another precipitous roll and a cascade of books toppled slowly over my floor, my bed and my helpless body. I scarcely felt this added insult. I just lay there rocking, rolling and retching, half buried under my entire library.

Suddenly there was a knock at the door and a panic stricken crew member burst into my cabin. 'I think Candice has dislocated her shoulder. We can't move her,' she explained. 'Can you come to C3 to check?'

I gasped in horror, my pallid features losing what little colour they had left. The C3 accommodation area was in the bowels of the ship. It sucked in the heat, diesel fumes and other special smells from the engine room like a sponge. Even on a calm sail it made me feel queasy.

My mind raced rapidly hunting for an excuse not to leave my comfortable refuge. Then I realized I didn't have a choice. After all this was just part of my duties as a doctor.

I grabbed my bucket, pushed through the untidy welter of books on my floor and staggered down the corridor toward Candice's cabin. Sure enough, in the simple act of turning over in bed, somehow, she had managed to dislocate her shoulder. She screamed when I touched her arm and strenuously resisted our attempts to walk her upstairs to the hospital.

We called for the emergency stretcher crew over the PA system and soon a most unlikely ambulance team appeared. Four burly deckmen in oilskins and shorts, muscled the stretcher through the cabin door. They had come straight from the watery chaos outside and dripped sea spray and salt over Candice as they hurriedly manhandled her onto the stretcher and upstairs to the hospital. I staggered along behind them clasping my faithful bucket by my side.

I surveyed our operating room in dismay. Boxes were slipping and sliding all over the place like participants in some crazy new dance. Anaesthetic machines and other equipment creaked and groaned, straining against the ropes that fortunately still held them secure. The emergency team had deposited Candice, still encased in her stretcher, on the floor inside the door and made a hasty retreat. She too was slipping with the motion and didn't look at all happy.

I called urgently for the emergency team again. We needed their strength to clear the operating table and work space. We reeled drunkenly around the room unearthing oxygen cylinders, instrument trays and other essential equipment from the chaos. Hurriedly we pushed aside boxes and heavy equipment that obstructed our efforts. Everything we moved joined the rock-and-roll party around us. Anxiously we watched the anaesthetic machine. If it broke loose and joined the party all our lives would be at risk.

By now the news of our medical emergency had spread throughout the ship and a hoard of eager spectators appeared, ostensibly to help. They knew my reputation and didn't believe their seasick doctor could possibly perform her medical duties in a storm. My performance staged on an unstable deck which pitched and rolled beneath me would be as good as any TV show.

Actually, this was not my first stormy adventure and I knew from experience I had about five minutes to work on resetting Candice's shoulder between interludes spent retching over my bucket.

Unfortunately, by this time, Candice was also sick and regrettably, her bouts of nausea didn't coincide with mine. As well as that, she was in considerable pain. She felt more comfortable sitting up, I wanted her to lie down. We argued, we used our buckets, we pitched and rolled with the motion, sidestepping the boxes which moved in slow motion around us. Our antics must have resembled those of an old Laurel and Hardy movie providing good entertainment for our gawking spectators.

We used our buckets again. We prayed. Finally in desperation, I decided to go ahead and try to insert an intravenous line, in spite of Candice's uncooperativeness. I bent over her arm and fought a rising wave of nausea. Miraculously, the needle slid straight into the vein and I quickly injected a muscle relaxant. Candice collapsed in a drugged stupor.

With one final bucket break I pulled on her shoulder and snapped it back into place. The audience cheered. Candice began to snore. The relaxant was working well and she was no longer seasick. I wished I could take some too.

With a sigh of relief I called the stretcher team again and they carried her peacefully sleeping form upstairs to the lounge to recover. I lurched back to my bed and collapsed in exhaustion. One of my friends appeared anxiously at my door. She was convinced the last stretcher team summons was for me, and expected to find my lifeless body in my room.

In retrospect, I can enjoy the humour of this and many other episodes of seasickness experienced during my years on board the *Anastasis*. However, at the time it was never pleasant.

This book is a story about how God can even use a chronically seasick Australian physician to make a little difference in the world. Welcome aboard to an adventure that will take us literally all over the world.

On this journey you will meet some fascinating people, visit some exotic places and see first-hand how God is at work in our world. You will become part of an unusual crew from over thirty different countries committed to sharing God's love.

Bon Voyage and don't forget those seasick pills!

Chapter 2

FROM THE ENDS
OF THE EARTH

> I took you from the ends of the earth, from its furthest corners I
> called you. I said, 'You are my servant: I have chosen you and
> have not rejected you.'
>
> Is 41:9

'Can I help you?' enquired the sandy haired young man watching me tentatively glance at each new arrival to Athens International Airport. It had not been a pleasant flight from New Zealand. For twenty-five hours I had sat uncomfortably upright, sandwiched between two rather large Greek bodies with a decidedly garlic aroma. On one side sat a plump, black-clad grandmother who smilingly pocketed the airline silverware after each meal. On the other was her amorous nephew who drank copious quantities of whisky and showered me with his unwanted attentions.

Now I was exhausted, bedraggled and anxious. The other passengers had left the airport two hours ago, yet I still sat there surrounded by a mountain of luggage. I felt like a small disoriented refugee – lost and lonely in the deserted lounge.

'No I am OK,' I assured him. 'Someone will be here to pick me up soon.' But to tell the truth I wasn't at all sure. I had no guarantee that my telex had arrived and was beginning to wonder if anyone was coming to collect me.

The situation seemed so bizarre and in many ways so unlike me. There was no way I could explain to this complete stranger that I was a medical doctor who had just left a successful practice in Christchurch New Zealand. And why? To travel halfway round the world to become a medical missionary on an old cruise liner that was being rehabilitated as a hospital ship. At present there wasn't even a functioning hospital on board and we didn't even know if it was feasible to build one. Worse still, I really didn't know much about Youth With A Mission (YWAM), the organization that had recruited me for this strange venture.

'Where are you going?', the young man persevered. 'Maybe I can help you contact your friends.'

I looked at him nervously. All I had was a phone number that didn't seem to work, and a post box number I obviously couldn't contact from the airport.

'I am here to join the *Anastasis*,' I told him hesitantly. 'It's a ship anchored somewhere out in the harbour.'

'Pyreus or Elevsis Harbour?' he shot back at me.

I stared at him blankly. It never occurred to me that Athens had more than one harbour. 'Well, I am not exactly sure,' I responded as the horror of my situation suddenly sank into my sleep-starved brain. Finding the *Anastasis* on my own could be like finding the proverbial needle in a haystack.

'Well if your friends don't turn up, give me a call,' he responded, handing me his phone number. He walked away with a very puzzled look.

'What in the world am I doing here? What have I gotten into?' I asked myself after he left. 'Here I am, half a world away from home, and I can't even find out where I am going.' I must be crazy. I always thought I was a sensible person. I rarely made rash and impulsive decisions. How could I give up the security of a good medical practice and a beautiful home in New Zealand to pursue such an uncertain future? Somewhere I must have made a mistake!

As I sat there, perched on top of my enormous mountain of luggage, I tried to reconstruct the past. What had motivated me to leave everything familiar and secure, to wind up lost and alone here in Greece?

It was now two years almost to the day since I first heard about the MV *Anastasis* from David and Linda Cowie. They bowled into my life in April 1979 while home on furlough and immediately caught my attention. David, tall and dark with boundless energy and a loud infectious laugh, was a striking contrast to Linda with her fair hair and quiet graciousness. Both were seasoned missionaries and spoke glowingly of the ship they were about to join. It was an old Italian cruise liner Youth With A Mission had just purchased to refit as a Christian Mercy Ship.

'It is a ship to serve the nations' they explained excitedly. 'A ship called *Anastasis* – the Greek word for "resurrection". One day we believe, this ship will bring new life to people throughout the world.' With sparkling eyes David and Linda enthusiastically detailed the plans to build a hospital on board. They pictured the ship ministering to the needs of the poor. There would be operations done on board, dental and medical teams to work in villages. The *Anastasis* would relieve suffering, offer health care, and build new homes. It would provide for the physical needs of people in the Third World while evangelism teams shared the Good News of God's love. My heart stirred in response.

David and Linda were on their way to Greece where the ship was presently undergoing repairs. They were part of the leadership team supervising the renovations. Now Youth With A Mission needed medical professionals to help establish the hospital and medical work.

From that moment I was somehow convinced that one day I would serve on the *Anastasis*. The mere thought of the ship excited me in a way that over-shadowed my more practical considerations. What did it matter that I succumbed to seasickness even in the calmest of weather? Or that I had no idea how to construct a hospital on a ship. That was not a skill they taught in medical school. They didn't even teach us much about Third World health care.

Never before had I felt so certain of God's direction for my life. I was ready to take the plunge and catch the next plane to Greece.

Really, now that I thought back, I could see that my decision wasn't impulsive at all. Even as a child, long before I became a Christian, I wanted to be a mission-ary doctor. I avidly devoured any missionary stories I could lay my hands on. Men and women like C T Studd, Paul Brandt, Gladys Aylward and Ida Scudder, some of the great missionary pioneers of our time, made indelible impressions on my mind. They inspired me with their dedication, courage and sacri-fice. I relished the stories they told of Africa and Asia often imagining myself in the primitive settings I read about.

From my own country, Australia, visions of the outback and Reverend John Flynn, the man who had conquered its remoteness through establishing the Flying Doctor Service and the Australia Inland Mission still thrilled my heart. He was a dreamer with the unquenchable will to make that dream come true. His perseverance and dedication were always a glowing example to me of the difference one human life can make when directed and guided by God.

In 1974 I graduated from Sydney University medical school hoping I would be able to serve as a physician overseas some day. However, I realized I needed experience first to develop confidence in my medical skills so that I really felt I had something constructive to offer.

For the next five years I worked in Christchuch, New Zealand, first as a resident at the local hospital and then in general practice. When I heard about the *Anastasis* in April 1979, I was just establishing my family practice and was leading an extremely comfortable life. I was preparing to buy a house and a new car and was no longer particularly enthralled with the idea of uprooting myself to some primitive and undeveloped part of the world.

However, I wasn't able to forget the *Anastasis*. My sense of calling deepened in spite of my efforts to suppress these promptings. I grew more and more restless and unsettled in the life I was leading. I bought a beautiful house high on the hill. Its magnificent view encompassed the river, the mountains and the ocean beyond. But it didn't seem to satisfy me. My deepest desire was still to somehow use my life to try and make a little difference in the world.

I smiled as I remembered the dilemma I faced.

How many people have to make a decision between missions and a brand new BMW, I wondered? And why on earth did I let missions win?

What really jolted my complacency, was an event that occurred about a year after my initial contact with David and Linda. By then I was praying about my future plans, but still dragging my feet.

One night, I was dining with friends who unbeknown to me spent several years working with Youth With A Mission. One of them suddenly asked, 'Have you ever considered joining the YWAM ship the *Anastasis*?' I gapèd in astonishment, choked on my mouthful of food and almost fell off my chair. I felt my inner thoughts were exposed. How did they know what I was struggling with? I didn't even realize they knew about the ship.

Their question was a clear milestone in my journey. Now I could no longer deceive myself. The comfortable life I led in New Zealand was not for keeps. I started to actively pursue joining YWAM and flying to the *Anastasis* in Greece.

Even after I made that landmark decision something within me protested and I struggled to follow through on my plan. In the next few weeks I often walked around my beautiful home weeping, grieving for the life, friends and material possessions I knew I was giving up. I resented the fact that none of my friends seemed called to make similar sacrifices. 'Why me, Lord?' I grumbled. 'Why am I the one who has to give everything up?'

I loved my medical practice too. Who would attend to the elderly people I visited every Wednesday afternoon? They plied me with interminable cups of tea, until I sloshed my way home in the evening. My visit was often their lifeline to the outside world. Who would visit them now and listen to their lonely complaints?

Or what of the old men at the Salvation Army Men's Home? The nurse told me that my visit was the highlight of their week. Hours before I arrived they spruced themselves up and vied for position on the footpath outside to watch my arrival. They discussed my clothes and always commented on any new outfit I appeared in. It brightened their day. My male medical colleagues didn't make the same impression. I always had twice as many patients as they did.

What lay ahead seemed so uncertain, too. I would receive no salary for my time on board, and at this point had virtually no assurance of financial support. I thought I had enough savings to last me a year, but no security beyond that.

Even my pursuit of the ship was fraught with uncertainty. It was difficult to obtain concrete information about where the *Anastasis* was and what it was doing. My enquiries about Youth With A Mission training schools met blank walls. My letters went unanswered and my questions multiplied. The path ahead was still shrouded in mystery. The *Anastasis* was little more than a hazy dreamlike image on the horizon.

What should I do? If I was leaving my practice I needed at least six months notice. 'What do I tell my patients?' I wondered. I was especially concerned about the pregnant women who wanted to be sure I would be there to deliver their babies. 'What do I tell my friends and my family? Surely they will think I am crazy.' The questions revolved chaotically in my mind, robbing my sleep, confusing my thoughts, magnifying my insecurity.

Surprisingly, the uncertainties strengthened my conviction that this was where I was heading and I decided to try a little experiment. When I first heard about the *Anastasis*, I sensed it would be two years until I was on board. Now I found myself needing to hold onto that conviction. I decided to take a risk based on the promptings of that inner urging and planned to close my practice and head to Greece in April 1981, exactly two years from the time of my initial contact.

The months passed and we moved into 1981. January and February went by and still no word from the *Anastasis*. Should I continue my preparations or should I wait? I agonized daily over my decision. 'Maybe my timing is wrong. Who am I after all to think that God will speak to me so specifically?'

My friends and colleagues too were concerned. 'Have you heard from that ship yet?' they often asked. 'Are you really leaving here in April? And where are you going anyway?' Their concerns fed my insecurities undermining my confidence in myself and my ability to hear God. I had so little tangible evidence to base my actions on. Never before had I been forced into such a blind walk of faith.

However, that still small voice grew more and more insistent. In spite of my doubts my sense of purpose increased. I was convinced that this was the right step for me. Whenever I prayed I felt at peace, assured that God had called me to the *Anastasis*. It was only when I moved my eyes onto the problem with its insurmountable obstacles that my faith wavered. In God's presence I was secure – away from that my mind was in turmoil.

Finally in the middle of March 1981, the long-awaited letter arrived. A training school was starting on board the *Anastasis* at the beginning of April. Could I come immediately to Greece? The letter had taken six weeks to reach me.

A whirlwind of activity followed. Only two weeks remained for my final preparations. No wonder I needed those inner assurances. I would arrive on the ship on April 1st, almost two years to the day from the time I first heard about the ministry. I laughed to myself as I realized it was also April Fools' Day, thinking that in this final plunge I really was showing what a fool I was.

These memories and many others flitted through my mind as I sat so disconsolately in the airport. It was now only four days since I closed my medical practice for the last time. And amazingly, in the last two weeks I had rented my house, disposed of my goods and given away my dog. My church leaders, who fully supported my decision, prayed for me and blessed my departure. I left surrounded by a crowd of friends who assembled at the airport to wish me bon voyage.

Now I was sitting in Greece, alone, still puzzled and more unsure than ever of the future. In my jet-lagged state I had no energy to move. I waited patiently for another two hours reminding myself to trust in God and not in circumstances.

Suddenly a harassed young man, with fair hair and blue eyes pushed through the airport doors. He peered around anxiously and whirled toward me frantically waving a sign in my direction. 'Are you Dr Chris Aroney?' he called. With a sigh of relief I stumbled toward this angel of mercy, glad that I was no longer alone.

'I was delayed in the traffic,' he explained as he wrestled with my luggage. 'Athens is a zoo.' And as we wended our way back through the narrow dusty streets I saw what he meant. Three lanes of traffic squeezed into the space for two. Impatient drivers honked their horns, gesticulating wildly at the mess. Some frustrated drivers even ignored the stop signs and sent pedestrians scampering in all directions as they roared through the intersections. Athens seemed to be a city in total chaos.

Then we arrived at the 'right' harbour – Elevsis – and loaded my bags into a rusty old launch that smelled strongly of diesel fuel and greasy rags. I gratefully clambered aboard and watched in mounting anticipation our approach to the *Anastasis*. It looked magnificent, framed by the craggy peaks of the island of Salamis behind. The sleek, 522 ft long hull, sparkled white and freshly painted against the blue of the Elevsis harbour. Sunlight danced off the proud green and blue smoke-stack adorned with the YWAM logo and from it, a thin wisp of smoke drifted lazily into the sky.

My arrival was like a dream come true. I struggled up the wobbly gangway into the welcoming arms of David and Linda Cowie. They introduced me to Don and Deyon Stephens, the ship's directors who greeted me with warm enthusiastic smiles.

I eyed them speculatively. They didn't look old enough to be in charge. Don had a round boyish face and straight black hair. Deyon was young and attractive with fair hair and fine features. However, they had directed the ministry since its inception in 1978 and now lived on board with their three young children. Their fourth child was born during their time in Greece.

I glanced around the reception area. The words from Isaiah 58:6–8, written in large gold letters, leapt out at me from one of the display cases beside the entrance.

> Is not this the kind of fasting I have chosen: to loose the chains of injustice and untie the cords of the yoke, to set the oppressed free and to break every yoke? Is it not to share your food with the hungry and to provide the poor wanderer with shelter – when you see the naked, to clothe him, and not to turn away from your own flesh and blood?

I gasped in amazement. These were my words. The ones God challenged me with back in 1970 when, as a new Christian, I first accepted the calling to missions. Now as I read these verses here on the walls of the *Anastasis* I knew I was in the right place. It was like coming home and I thanked God for the guidance that had led me so wonderfully to that place. I still wasn't sure of what lay ahead, but I was convinced God would be with me in this adventure, each step of the way.

Chapter 3

NEEDLE GUNS AREN'T FOR SISSIES

> Consider it pure joy, my brothers, when ever you face trials of
> many kinds, because you know that the testing of your faith
> develops perseverance. Perseverance must finish its work so
> that you may be mature and complete, not lacking anything.
> Jas 1:2–4

The generator beneath my bed rumbled into life at 5.30 in the morning shattering my sleep. Like some gigantic sea creature emerging from the deep, its presence invaded the whole ship. It shook me into life and forced me to face the day ahead.

I buried my head in the pillow and groaned. I did not want to get up. It was now almost twelve months since my arrival, and we were still sitting in the harbour in Greece renovating the ship.

It wasn't Greece I objected to. I loved it. For me, this was not just another country to explore or one in which to wait while the ship was prepared, it was part of my cultural heritage, the land of my ancestors. My father's family migrated to Australia from Greece in the early 1920s and now I had a wonderful opportunity to explore the nation from which they came. What a special gift from God.

Athens particularly intrigued me with its conglomeration of ancient and modern architecture. The Acropolis dominated the skyline. It soared majestically atop a pinnacle of craggy dark rocks and at night glittered, vivid and almost unreal in the stark spotlights. Around its base, the narrow twisted thoroughfares of the old city wended their way between low houses with cracked and decaying plaster, capped with gently sloping tiles. Heavy balconies overhung the footpaths of worn and half-sunken flagstones. Numerous little food shops bulged with tempting arrays of cheese and olives and bread. Tourist stores weighed down and overflowing with brass and ceramic ornaments beckoned the unwary traveller.

A short distance away, around Constitution Square, wide modern roadways and smart new shops bespoke a different world. Immense hotels and commercial buildings pressed in on the spacious square. Here larger cafes set out chairs and tables under brightly coloured awnings on the broad pavement. Tourists sat and relaxed after hectic excursions amongst the ruins.

Delphi, a dusty three-hour bus trip away, was another wonderful delight. It clung precariously to a steep sloping hillside with one of nature's most startling views rolling mile upon mile before it. Blue-shadowed mountains beyond red-flowered fields brooded over a narrow wooded valley that plunged deep down to a glimpse of the sea far below. Above the town rose the ancient amphitheatre with its layer upon layer of ruins. The first flight of stairs in the Sacred Way climbed between the sanctuaries, the half fallen columns of small temples, the pedestals of statues and the monuments, until high up, in the centre of the vast arena, it reached the ruined Temple of Apollo. Above the temple, at the topmost rim, stood the theatre and beyond that stretching along the sky line, and hidden by trees and bushes, the exhausted walker came upon the stadium where the athletes had competed.

I explored this ancient land with great enthusiasm, revelling in the wonder of its incredible history. I imagined my ancestors as part of the ancient culture I was exploring.

The *Anastasis* too was all I had hoped for. She was a beautiful ship, there was no doubt about that. Built in Trieste, Italy in the early 1950s she exhibited all the elegance and style of a high class Italian lady. Swirling orange and white Venetian glass lamps studded the meeting rooms, their soft glow gently illuminating the beautiful wooden etchings around the walls. Larger than life size murals, depicting exotic hunting scenes, looked down majestically over the dining rooms. The reception area was broad and spacious, with a beautiful elegant staircase climbing graciously to the deck above.

Beneath the surface unfortunately, was another story. The engine room was thick with dirt and grime and required a complete overhaul. The hull sported layer upon layer of old paint, mottled with unsightly patches of brown rust. Cranes hung dead and silent over the cargo holds, their mechanisms corroded by salt and sea air. A smell of must and mould shrouded the cabins that had stood unused for years and everything in sight seemed to need repairs. There was little money and even less fuel.

Most difficult of all for me, the medical ministry was still little more than a dream. Most of my time was spent performing the hard physical labour necessary to renovate the hospital. There was so much work to do and very few people to do it. Perhaps the *Anastasis* would never sail, the locals certainly doubted it.

Conditions on board were not exactly what I expected either and the last twelve months had been a real struggle. We frugally conserved money in every possible way. For instance, the generators were switched off at ten o'clock at night and after that we groped our way around in the dark silent tomb. No electricity meant not only no light, but no water as well. Often the hot water was turned off for even longer periods. Sometimes it only came on for an hour a day – what we called 'the hour of power for a shower'.

Then there was the plumbing system. It made early morning bathroom visits a real nightmare. With the electricity off at night, air accumulated in the pipes, creating large pressurized bubbles which lurked around the toilet, waiting to explode with great gusto whenever I flushed it in the morning. Water, toilet paper and other unmentionables sprayed in all directions. Sometimes I had to clean the ceiling afterwards. It was almost enough to make me book my plane ticket home.

I looked around my tiny six by eight foot cabin in despair. It was the largest cabin on board allocated to a single person but still looked very cramped and uninviting. I slept at one end in a narrow bunk bed with a lumpy, elderly mattress that also provided my only sitting area. At the other end stood a small wooden dressing table with a mirror over it. It was flanked by more of those beautiful old Venetian lights decorated with orange swirls. Here, they tinged everything with a sickly yellow glow that only made the room look worse.

At the foot of my bed, the single porthole provided a small circle of light which did nothing to improve the dingy grey of the bulkheads and worn out linoleum. My poor philodendron struggled manfully to survive beneath it. Outside there was a beautiful view – a magnificent expanse of blue water studded with disabled ships. However it was totally inaccessible, the porthole was six feet up the bulkhead and set into a twelve inch deep alcove. Luckily, I had my own bathroom with a small shower, wash basin and toilet, and really had much to be grateful for. Most of the other single people shared cabins, sometimes with two or three people. Often these rooms were not much larger than my own.

My list of complaints appeared endless. I shuddered at the mere thought of the hospital, my first tour of which left me in a state of shock. No self-respecting medical professional would ever consider working there. The doctor's office and operating area occupied a single room. It was bleak and austere with a tiled floor, bare metal bulkheads and metal furniture, all at least thirty years old and built to last forever. In one corner stood a beaten up old glass topped desk and chair, and on the bulkhead facing, an ancient glass fronted instrument cabinet. Most of its contents were worn, rusty and obsolete. Under the portholes stood two old-fashioned porcelain wash sinks, and an antiquated, narrow operating table overhung by a single 150 watt bulb straddled the centre of the room. Even the simplest surgical procedure was challenging. Modern technology had obviously passed this hospital by.

Behind the surgery were a minute pharmacy and lab. The pharmaceuticals would have looked great in a museum. Ancient bottles of morphine, obviously the ship's original supplies from the 1950s, pills and powders I could only guess at the use of, and even a bottle of Cognac, for medicinal purposes only, of course, all adorned the shelves. Everything was labelled in Italian, or if it had arrived on board more recently, in German or French or Swedish. My brain sizzled with the efforts of translation.

Down the white tiled corridors on either side of the surgery, were the four wards with a total of eighteen beds – narrow double decker bunks with hardly enough space for a small person to squeeze between. I had nightmarish visions of patients tumbling head-long out of the top bunks in the middle of a storm. This certainly bore little resemblance to my ideas of a hospital, even a missionary hospital.

The facilities obviously needed extensive renova-tion and I soon realized it was the medical depart-ment's responsibility to accomplish that. And the only way to see a fully functional hospital on the ship was to build it ourselves.

I groaned again and turned over in my narrow bunk. 'Twelve months on board' I thought. 'And so little to see for it.' I was never meant to be a carpenter.

At least we now lived on board. Shortly after I joined the crew, the Greek authorities asked the ship's community to move ashore. They doubted that our renovations would ever be complete and decided to bury the *Anastasis* in a part of the Elevsis Harbour known as 'the graveyard'.

Rows of ships, some just resting for the winter, oth-ers derelict and forlornly awaiting the cutting torch, crisscrossed the area. The *Anastasis* was the first in a line of ten ships trussed tightly together, like sardines in a can. Beside us stood an enormous old liner called the *Nogos*. Rich furnishings, reminiscent of a bygone age, were shrouded in heavy covers and its opulent rooms stood silent and cold as a tomb. Its sombre shadow hung over us like an oppressive dark cloud that robbed the *Anastasis* of the last vestiges of sunshine. We stood cold, dark and miserable at its side. Chances were it would soon become scrap metal. For the *Nogos* this was truly the graveyard. Many of the local people thought it would be ours too.

Only a skeleton crew worked on board during the *Anastasis* sojourn in the graveyard. The deck and engine room staff divided into two teams of twenty to twenty-five people who alternated weeks on board. Every second week I was part of the team that crossed the harbour from our winter home ashore to labour on board. As the only medical person on our team I spent many long lonely hours in the hospital, chipping and scraping. I only emerged from my cold, silent world for coffee breaks and meals. Even the evenings were bleak and uninviting. The generators shut down at 5pm, and for the rest of the night we huddled around a solitary electric light in the dining room. We played cards or watched and rewatched our meagre supply of videos.

I struggled abysmally through those depressing days. They were probably some of the most difficult of my life, not only physically, but spiritually and emotionally as well.

Many of my struggles revolved around a ghastly instrument called a needle gun. It is commonly used on ships to remove rust and old paint from metal bulkheads. This diabolical instrument resembles an unwieldy twelve pound gun, and acts like a miniature hand-held jack-hammer. Dozens of small needles protrude through the gun barrel and vibrate noisily back and forth under the power of compressed air as the needle gun greedily eats at the rust.

A cacophony of sound exploded through the ship each time I set to work, isolating me from the surrounding world. Paint chips, dust and dirt spewed in all directions whenever I operated it. The debris penetrated my hair, my clothes and even my mouth and eyes. I protected myself from complete annihilation by wearing old overalls, ear muffs, goggles and a mask to cover my face. Bandages wrapped around my wrists to dampen the vibrations completed the picture. I sometimes felt like a monster from outer space.

Over the six months the ship was in the graveyard, I spent what seemed like endless days encased in the world the needle gun created. I hated the feeling of being totally alone. My arms ached constantly from the vibrations and weight of the instrument. I was always dirty and covered in dust.

The work progressed slowly and painfully. It took weeks to strip the paint from each room. My only satisfaction was the perverse pleasure I gained in watching those pernicious rust spots and countless layers of paint disappear. They represented the enemies I was fighting both inside and out. They held no place in any well-organized hospital and I attacked them as if they were some vicious infectious disease.

When the needle gunning was completed, I started sanding and painting. That was no easier. We were so short of money that each sheet of sandpaper was used until every single grain of sand was ground away. Sometimes I sanded my fingers raw as I endeavoured to eke out our inadequate supplies. I wore band-aids on all my fingers, multiple layers of them. I often wondered if my fingers would ever recover. I doubted I would ever regain enough sensitivity to adequately examine another medical patient.

Fortunately I was not alone in this mammoth task. Doug and Kathryn Mar had arrived to head up the medical team on board the ship just two weeks before I became a crew member. However, because we alternated our weeks on the ship while it was in the graveyard, we rarely spent time together.

The Mars both made a deep and enduring impression on my life during the years we spent together. Doug was unusually tall for someone of Chinese ancestry. His gold-rimmed spectacles and black moustache endowed him with a permanently serious and thoughtful look that was intensified by his constant questioning and hunting for answers. Doug trained as a physician in Berkeley, California, but his skills and interests extended far beyond his medical training. He always wanted to know how and why things worked and spent long hours creating new gadgets or examining old ones.

On one occasion a crew member injured her knee and required a knee-brace. There were none available, so Doug spent long hours in the welding shop manufacturing his own. It was a piece of art, with beautifully moulded padded casings for the thigh and calf and specially made hinges to maintain the movement of the knee. We were all very proud of his ingenuity.

Kathryn was his exact opposite. She was petite and

fair haired, and grew up in Georgia in the Southern United States. She presented all the outward fragility of a Southern Belle, but could hold her own with a needle gun or paint brush and was also a very competent nurse practitioner. Kathryn had a deeply compassionate heart and glowed with an inner resilience and spiritual maturity that quickly put both Doug and I in our places. It was she who always reminded us to pray when we were carried away by 'more practical' considerations.

Before joining the *Anastasis*, Doug and Kathryn worked with the Khymer refugees on the Thai/Cambodian border. They knew intimately the effects of the heartache and despair experienced by people who lived through unbelievable atrocities. Their lives changed radically because of the suffering and anguish they witnessed. Their experiences fuelled their desire to see the ship used as a vessel to help needy people. I listened avidly as they shared their stories, a growing ache in my own heart. Like them I too wanted to use my skill to help people in physical and spiritual need.

That hope still seemed like an impossible dream, however, a vague idea at the back of our minds. For now, the hospital construction was all the reality we could cope with. It stretched our faith to even believe we would one day have a functional facility. It was almost impossible to pray for a hospital that would perform all kinds of medical and surgical work when we did not even have enough money to buy a new box of band-aids, or when our only surgical instruments were thirty years old.

It was Doug's ingenuity and perseverance that kept us working during that initial tedious renovation time. His alert, inventive mind was an endless source of new ideas for creative gadgets to make our job easier. For example, his needle gun holder, relieving the strain of this unpleasant task for Kathryn and I, was a marvel to all the ship's crew.

Neither Kathryn nor I are exactly built on Amazonian lines. Kathryn weighs in at 110 lb, and I at 120. The needle guns were just too heavy for our puny strength. Our arms ached with the effort of trying to hold them up to the overheads. No amount of willpower could overcome the weakness of our bodies. Yet there was no other help available. Without our assistance, Doug would have to perform all the heavy manual work himself, a job which was obviously beyond him.

After several days of brainstorming and feverish activity in the carpenter's shop, Doug proudly appeared with his latest invention. It was an old wooden stool to which he had attached a plank of wood three feet long, three inches wide and an inch deep. This extension pivoted on the seat of the stool and the needle gun was securely strapped at the far end. Doug devised a trigger mechanism at the other end to operate the gadget. This crude invention was well within our capabilities to manoeuvre and we greeted it with all the respect due any mighty new technological advance. Now the work could go on.

As the winter approached another hazard developed. I was born with an internal thermostat that functions best in the 80–90°F range. Winter is always a miserable time for me. But the cold blast of air emitted by the needle gun intensified my suffering. It penetrated deep into my bones, numbing my fingers and stiffening my joints. A constant chilling ache per-vaded my body. Half a dozen layers of clothing made no difference. I knew I would never be warm again. My only solace was to curl up in bed at night snuggling close to my hot water bottles and covering myself with a mountain of blankets.

It just didn't seem fair. Why did I have to go through all of this? After all, I was a doctor not a construction expert. My years of medical training and practice had certainly not prepared me for needle guns and sandpapering. They just didn't teach such skills at medical school, and if they had I think I would have chosen another profession.

I often found myself arguing silently with God. 'Lord I am a doctor,' I reminded him, muttering to myself at his seeming failure to recognize this fact. 'I am not qualified to chip and paint and scrape walls. Also Lord I don't like doing it. Isn't there some other way to prepare this ministry?' I asked. Letters from friends and family confirmed my belief. Nobody should expect me to do the things that occupied most of my day.

Spiritually it was a time of real struggle and much needed growth for me. I was often confused and continually questioned my faith. As I chipped and sanded, scraping away the rust and layers of paint God also chipped and scraped away at my life. There were many layers of 'paint' that I needed removed as well. At times I felt a needle gun was being used on me too. And I didn't really appreciate it. Not only was the ship in the graveyard, I felt that I was too.

'What does it really mean for me to be a Christian?' I often pondered. 'What kinds of commitments am I willing to make to follow Christ?' That seemed to be the bottom line. As long as life was comfortable and my career such an integral part of my Christian walk, as long as I enjoyed doing what God was asking of me, it had been so easy to follow Christ. Now I was not so sure.

'Are you willing to follow me no matter where I lead you?' I sensed God was saying to me. 'Are you willing to trust me even when you cannot clearly see what lies ahead?' 'Will you obey me even if you are never able to practise medicine again?' The questions hammered at my mind, echoed in the hammering of the needle gun. 'But I am a doctor,' I continually reminded him. 'I don't want to give that up.'

Other questions too pressed around me. What, I wondered, are the really important things in my life? Looking back over the past few years I saw no clear answers and knew that now I desperately needed them.

Having entered medical school as a Christian I found my studies to be a delightful revelation of God's creation. I loved anatomy, and biochemistry, and often felt awe at the intricate nature of the body they revealed. To me they reflected the intricacy of the character of our heavenly Father. We are truly fearfully and wonderfully made and I rejoiced in this discovery.

As a result of my knowledge and my understanding of God's presence in all I studied, medicine became extremely important to me. It was a delight to practise a profession in which I found so much joy and satisfaction. I loved my work and could see no better way to serve God. To be a medical missionary seemed a natural extension of this direction.

Now suddenly I was stripped of all that seemed important to me. My past achievements no longer mattered. My skills and profession were unimportant. In my limited understanding I thought I came to the ship to be a missionary doctor, to use my skills and training to reach out and help others. Now I was learning God's purposes were far more complex.

Spiritually I had reached a crisis point. In the midst of my struggles with the needle gun, I sensed some of God's deeper purposes in bringing me to Greece. He was not interested in me because of my profession or talents. It didn't really matter if I never practised medicine again. What really mattered was my relationship to him and my ability to trust his guidance, even when the path ahead looked rocky and forbidding.

I suspect that instant success is rarely in God's plan for us. In fact I doubt that he really considers success as we measure it to be very important at all. It was the hardships and struggles I experienced that contributed most to my character and developed my trust in God. My years of chipping paint and sanding walls taught me the value of obedience and perseverance. I learned to trust in God in ways I never had before and developed important foundations that were invaluable to the ministry itself.

As my pilgrimage continued through long hours of physical toil with little scope for my medical skills, I became aware of how easily I was caught up by the lure of outward success, in spite of the fact that it bore no relationship to the really important things of Christian life. Like so many in the medical profession, much of my value lay in what I did and not who I was. It had also been so important in my world, to pass exams and to show myself successful in my work and profession.

Now these values had lost their importance and I began to see more clearly God's measure of value. Success in God's eyes lies in obedience, perseverance and trust. And he was instilling this in all of us on board. Unfortunately I realized there was no short cut method to acquire them.

Over these difficult months in the graveyard, my responses began to change. I was stripped of my pride and independence bringing me closer and closer to the realization that without God and the grace he showers upon all of us, our endeavours produce nothing but hay and stubble of no lasting value in eternity.

Looking at the past, I realized I had an incredible foundation to build my faith on too. There was so much to trust in. I looked back with joy remembering the way God led me to the ship and how he continued to provide not only for my daily needs but for those of all the community. Even just being here in Greece was the fulfilment of a dream for me. I had always wanted to travel especially to visit the lands of my ancestors and here I was, spending an extended period in the very country my father's people came from.

There were some areas however in which trust was always difficult. I left New Zealand with what seemed like adequate support for at least the first twelve months away. In the ensuing months the New Zealand dollar devalued sharply. Suddenly I didn't have enough money to provide for even my basic needs. I could not afford a new tube of toothpaste or a bottle of shampoo.

Out of the blue, anonymous gifts started to appear in the mail. Sometimes there would be an envelope with a few dollars; in others a more substantial cheque. All came from other members of the ship's crew most of whom had very little more money than I did. It was very humbling to be so cared for by others and to be totally reliant on them. It was special too, to sense the love and concern that generated such gifts. This was an amazing and very special group of people, a true community of God's family. We not only lived together, we also shared our resources and supported each others' struggles as well.

God loves us even in the graveyard, I realized. He cares about us and all our needs, no matter how insignificant. He is interested in us not because of what we do for him but because of who he is. I slowly began to see that I could trust God no matter what he asked me to do. I was God's child and he would always be faithful to me. I needed to be faithful to him too, no matter how unpleasant I found the roadway ahead.

One event that helped me gain perspective in my struggles was a message preached during my first Easter on board. It fitted so aptly into the 'graveyard' experiences both I and the ship endured. The speaker talked about the meaning of 'Anastasis' or 'Resurrection' and reminded us that there can be no resurrection without an experience of death. Death of course is not only painful, it is also smelly. Lazarus spent four days in the tomb. When Christ asked for the stone in front of the tomb to be moved away Martha responded 'by this time there is a bad odour' (Jn 11:39).

I often felt like that during my time in Greece. It was as though I had died to the past and my aspirations as a doctor, and was waiting like Lazarus and like the *Anastasis*, for the resurrection of my life. At times I felt a bad odour surrounding me and all of us struggling to get out of the tomb.

While the ship was in the graveyard, most of the crew and their families lived at Kinnetta Beach Bungalows, half-way between Athens and Corinth. On the outside this resort was as attractive as any you would ever see on an exotic tourist brochure. Whitewashed bungalows, festooned with scarlet bougainvillaea and surrounded by ageing gnarled olive trees, dotted the property. They squatted low by the beach looking out toward the sparkling waters of the Mediterranean.

Inside the hotel was a mess. A recent earthquake had made some areas uninhabitable, and left the rest with peeling plaster, gaping cracks and insecure fixtures. It was no longer fit for tourists to live in but was a perfect place for 150 displaced missionaries.

Each day brought some new adventure. Shortly after our arrival one of my friends was innocently brushing his teeth when the sink he was using suddenly fell off the wall. He shouted for his room-mate and held on desperately to prevent the pipes from breaking. Water sprayed everywhere as he grappled with the load. It was several minutes before the water supply was cut off saving him from his crazy predicament.

Sometimes the electric plugs fell out of the wall when we tried to use them. On other occasions just plugging in a kettle fused all the lights. We never knew what to expect.

The hotel would have been great fun in the summer, but our arrival coincided with the start of cold weather. Those bungalows were definitely only fair weather habitations. Concrete blocks and cement floors stored and exuded the cold air. The large sliding glass doors at the front of each unit provided maximum light and sun in the summer, but the wind now whistled and whirled through their gaping cracks with great ferocity. We taped sheets of plastic across the doors and windows in a somewhat futile attempt to stay the icy blasts.

The heating system was just as impractical. No central heating here. A single inefficient and ancient radiator exuded a small circle of heat that made little difference to the room's frigid temperatures. In the morning we sat huddled on our beds wrapped in sleeping bags. We removed the heater's safety guards and hovered over the glowing element toasting our bread on forks. It was definitely more effective as a toaster than a heater.

Only Ruth and Cheryl, the great companions I shared my beach bungalow with, made Kinetta bearable. Cheryl Robertson and I were often mistaken for sisters. At 5ft 8in she was a good inch taller than I was. We both had short black hair, though hers had a beautiful natural wave I envied. We both grew up racing after brothers who taught us to be tomboys, and we both knew how to be blunt and determined. Even vocationally we shared many similarities. Cheryl was a nurse and spent her early days on board cleaning in the hospital. Now she worked with the Discipleship Training School programme. However, when we opened our mouths it was obvious we came from different parts of the world. Cheryl spoke with a wonderful rich South African accent.

Our other companion was Ruth Crow from England. She combined the elegance and grace of the

British upper class with a wonderful gift for hospitality and entertaining. Ruth was quieter, gentler and more mellow than her straightforward colonial friends. However, she shared our love for adventure and was always first to volunteer when some crazy exploit beckoned. Ruth spoke French fluently and had even done her nurse's training in Paris. She could also converse in German and to a lesser extent Greek, and was a great companion on a trip into Athens or even around the world.

We all soon became close friends willingly sharing our belongings and our lives. First person awake in the morning turned on the electric kettle and made the tea, an important ritual for those of us with British ancestry. Then donning the warmest garment available, usually my sheepskin coat, this hardy individual (mostly Cheryl), headed across the chilly courtyard to get breakfast.

None of us had much money during the time at Kinetta. Often we pooled our last pennies (or drachmas in Greek currency) to buy a treat such as a carton of yoghurt or a Greek pastry. Even simple pleasures like this seemed more special when we were all scraping the bottom of the barrel to make them possible.

We shared all aspects of our lives. We studied the Bible together or prayed for each other. We shared times of fasting, and feasting. We shared news from home and hopes for the future. We shared our struggles and our frustrations regarding the ministry. On one occasion while Ruth was away, we moved a patient into our bungalow to occupy her empty bed. We didn't have any other hospital facilities available. Cheryl and I became the medical attendants on duty.

Cheryl willingly shared not only her nursing skills but her home as well.

In spite of its difficulties Kinetta Beach Bungalows held many fond memories too. I look back on my stay there as a time of joy rather than hardship. I particularly enjoyed the celebrations within the community. We were constantly planning parties and festivities. Even a package from home was cause for celebration – particularly if it contained edible goodies.

The highlight of these celebrations for me was the wedding of my friends, Philip and Carla. Philip Rooke hailed from South Africa. His rugged features and wide-based swaggering gait distinguished him as one of the few seasoned sailors in the community. He was always cheerful with a broad mischievous grin, and once had the audacity to throw me into the Mediterranean fully clothed. Carla was a true missionary kid. Born in the US, she spent much of her childhood in India. There was no way the hardships of Greece could throw a dampener over her enthusiastic preparations.

I love sewing, and agreed to make her wedding dress unaware of what I was letting myself in for. First, we braved the tiny Greek material shops with mountainous stacks of fabric crammed into their depths. The piles teetered precariously each time we touched them. Occasionally we precipitated an avalanche as we rummaged around. The shop attendants gesticulated wildly and impatiently as we deliberated and grinned broadly when we made our decisions.

For a pattern I used an old nightdress vaguely resembling the style Carla wanted. I picked it to pieces to figure out how it was made, then crossed my fingers and prayed the finished product would look similar. The patient in Ruth's bed sewed lace around the skirt's train. Amazingly, the result of this rather strange community effort fitted the bride perfectly.

The whole community participated fully in the preparations for this and all celebrative events. Some of the women wandered the verges of the highways picking armfuls of vibrantly coloured wildflowers to decorate the hall. The cooks prepared a special meal of exotic but inexpensive Greek delicacies. And all of us used our creativity to make special little gifts for the bride and groom. The old terracotta yoghurt containers for example, were painted to make beautiful fruit bowls or vases.

On the day of the wedding, the bridesmaids danced down the aisle in colourful, flowing gowns strewing fragrant petals in their path. The bride followed behind, tall and regal in her homemade gown. Flowers adorned her auburn hair and she glowed radiantly as she took Philip's hand and they exchanged their vows. I could not imagine a more splendid wedding. It was a wonderful time of joy and celebration that reflected the tremendous sense of closeness and family that was so much a part of our community.

The Greeks too loved to celebrate and we willingly participated, especially at Easter time. This was the highlight of their religious calendar and already held special significance for us because of the name of the ship. Days beforehand, barbecue spits were erected in backyards, along the footpaths, wherever a family could find space. Fires were kindled to await the great day. The crowded little blue and white houses bulged at the seams as family members gathered from all over the country to join in the festivities.

Everyone rose at the crack of dawn on Easter Sunday morning. The women set to work preparing mountains of Greek salad with fresh feta cheese, sun ripened tomatoes and olives. Delicious herb-covered potatoes roasted in the ovens and sweet Greek pastries dripping in honey were set out on enormous platters. The men lit the fires and the barbecues soon glowed with red-hot coals. A whole lamb firmly trussed to a pole was lowered onto the spit. It had to be lamb, in remembrance of Christ our Paschal lamb. Each member of the family helped turn the spit and baste the animal

By the afternoon, delicious smells of garlic, thyme and roasted lamb wafted around us as we walked by and we stopped to savour the wonderful aromas. The families looked up with cries of 'Ella, ella! (Come, come!).' They welcomed everyone. This was a time for open hospitality, a reminder of the fact that Christ welcomes all of us into his family. Soon we too were sitting around the magnificent feast. Shouts of 'Christo anasti (Christ is risen)' brought from us the response 'Allythos anasti' (He is risen indeed)' as we all rejoiced together in the memory of our risen Saviour.

Even today, as I celebrate Easter I am reminded of that scene. 'Christ is risen – Christo anasti' is, for me, not only symbolic of the resurrection of Christ. It is also a reminder of the work God did both in my life and in the ship, the *Anastasis*, during those days in the graveyard.

Chapter 4

FROM GRAVEYARD TO RESURRECTION

Jesus called in a loud voice, 'Lazarus, come out!' The dead man came out, his hands and feet wrapped with strips of linen, and a cloth around his face. Jesus said to them, 'Take off the grave clothes and let him go.'

Jn 11:43–44

It was while the ship was in the graveyard and we lived at Kinetta Beach Bungalows, that one of the most amazing incidents of our sojourn in Greece occurred. Perhaps God was showing us that he was part of our celebrations too and wanted to encourage us that our 'anastasis', our resurrection, was on the way.

It all began with our desperate desire to see the ship leaving Greece, fully repaired and equipped for the ministry ahead. Things had never seemed more desperate. Our coffers were empty and the renovation work progressed very slowly. Youth With A Mission had owned the ship for more than three years and it still hadn't entered into ministry. From a human standpoint the road ahead looked bleak and forbidding. Some members of the community left, confused and depressed by our lack of progress. The rest of us found the pathway arduous and often unpleasant.

Finally in October 1981, as a response to our grim situation, we organized a period of prayer and fasting. Over a forty day span, each person within the community took several days to pray and fast. We developed a roster to make sure every day over that forty days was well covered with prayer focused on asking God for clear direction concerning the future of the ministry.

Early each morning we met for a time of community prayer led by Deyon Stephens. The whole community congregated in a room that looked out over the Mediterranean Sea. The water was usually calm and untroubled in the early morning light and lapped gently against the pebble beach in front of us.

One morning, almost at the end of the forty day period, our prayer meeting was in progress, when suddenly our attention was distracted. Flashes of silver like sunlight suddenly erupted from the water and cascaded in a brilliant stream of light onto the beach. I gazed in fascination at the unusual sight, unable at first to comprehend its significance.

Suddenly a ripple of excitement spread across the room. 'The fish are jumping,' someone shouted and we all raced outside to witness the amazing display. For about 150 yards in front of our hotel, there were fish throwing themselves out of the water. Some leapt several feet into the air before they landed at our feet. Others flopped in exhausted puddles around us. They lay stranded in gasping wriggling heaps all along the water's edge. It was an incredible sight.

The children, dismissed from their school classes, enthusiastically joined our efforts, squealing with delight as they watched the fish leaping and splashing around us. Don Stephens tried to throw one back but it jumped straight out again. He stood at the water's edge, a fish in each hand and a broad grin on his face. It was like a miracle and he led us in a prayer of rejoicing and thanksgiving on the spot.

We marshalled our resources, assembling wheelbarrows, buckets, plastic bags and any other receptacles we could find. Chattering excitedly, we all scurried round the beach, peering into pools and behind rocks, to capture the miraculous harvest. We dragged our catch toward the kitchen and began counting. How incredible it was. Over 8000 fish stranded themselves on the beach that day. The local people came and stared in amazement – they had never seen anything like it before.

We prayed and rejoiced and sang, marvelling at the incredible way God answered our prayers for direction. None of us ever expected anything this spectacular or unusual. What an incredible indication that God was still with us. It seemed symbolic of a promise of things to come, a promise of the abundant harvest we would one day see from the *Anastasis*. We felt God was assuring us of his blessing on our ministry and it gave us new hope for the future.

Amazingly, our chief cook happened to be a Norwegian. That seemed like a miracle too. He knew exactly how to prepare and preserve those fish and soon had us all working hard cleaning our catch.

Much to my disgust, as I discovered over the next few days, miracles often have a negative side as well as a positive one, and require quite a bit of effort on our part to accomplish. It takes a long time and a lot of people to gut and clean over 8000 fish. Everyone played a part.

We pulled the dining tables together and set up a

rather smelly production line. It was hard to maintain our enthusiasm as we gutted, salted and preserved our harvest. Soon we all reeked with the smell and our hands ached from using inadequate implements. We didn't have enough sharp knives. I noticed Linda Cowie using her sewing scissors to cut open the fish. One of the school children pinched her nose as she worked, trying fruitlessly to avoid the smell. It was a very unpleasant aromatic experience but I wouldn't have missed it for the world.

As we processed the fish I learned a very important lesson. I realized, with horror, how easily our rejoicing could turn to grumbling. It made me think of the children of Israel in the desert. All of us have the potential to be like them, I surmised, and God's provision, if not handled with gratitude can look like a curse. It took days to adequately clean up our catch and they formed a supplement to our diet for many months to come. By the time they were finished some of the crew were heartily sick of our 'miracle fish'. It was hard to remember the excitement of the miracle and God's abundant generosity in a slim season.

The time in the graveyard passed very slowly. Work progressed at a snail's pace as our meagre teams of twenty workers continued to alternate back and forth to the ship. One week of hard, frantic lonely activity on board then one of relaxation, with little work to do back at the hotel. It was a strange surreal existence.

Then, in February 1982, the ship was finally ready to sail out of that dismal graveyard. With great anticipation we planned a momentous trip of three miles to our new berth. The *Anastasis* would sail from the graveyard in Elevsis Harbour to the Chandris ship-

yard on the island of Salamis. We all desperately
wanted to be on board for this auspicious occasion.

Much to my delight I realized my team was the
privileged crew assigned to the ship that week. The
rest of the community watched our departure with
envy.

The night before the ship was due to sail our anticipation ran high. For most of us this trip, short though
it was, marked our first experience of sailing on the
Anastasis. The joy of throwing off the graveyard
shrouds added to our excitement.

That evening, the captain called us together for a
special announcement. 'Tomorrow we have a large
group of local Christians coming to join us while we
sail,' he said. 'These people have been some of our
most constant supporters during our stay in Greece
and I hope that you will all treat them kindly and
with consideration.'

All of us sat in stunned silence for a moment, trying
desperately to think of where these supporters could
possibly come from. None of us had any ideas. We
only had a few local supporters none of whom would
be particularly interested in watching our short
though significant trip.

Then with a grin he added, 'You married men had
better clean your cabins too.' The light dawned. He
was talking about the families at Kinetta. The community was coming home!

We erupted into loud cheering awed and amazed
by God's timing. Everyone would be there to see the
ship emerge from the graveyard. We could rejoice
together at the marvel of our resurrection.

The families arrived early the next morning in a
fleet of crowded launches. Chubby infants, bundled

in parkas and hats to guard against the bitter cold, were handed through the engine room portholes. It was too dangerous to carry them up the treacherous B-deck ladder. Older children clung desperately to the ropes as they edged up the side of the ship. An adult crew member followed closely behind to protect their ascent. Then came the pregnant women, who manoeuvred themselves awkwardly on board, determined not to miss this wonderful occasion.

The following day two bustling tugs nosed alongside and pushed and prodded until the *Anastasis* slowly inched its way out from beside the *Nogos*. The Greek pilot, black hair blown into thick strands by the breeze, stood on the wing directing the operation. Don Stephens and the captain stood beside him, hovering protectively over the proceedings.

Families lined the decks in excited huddles, watching our departure. We all sang and clapped and cheered as the deckies threw the lines overboard and severed our links to the graveyard. One of the galley staff stood out on the aft deck playing his trumpet, oblivious to the hustle and bustle of our departure. The triumphant notes of 'Up From the Grave He Arose' rang throughout the *Anastasis* as we pulled free from the other vessels. Exultantly we shed our shroud and emerged into the brilliant sunlight. We were off, sailing to our new berth and to a new life. Bursting with joy we left behind the place that many thought would be our tomb.

The *Anastasis* exploded into new life. The decks and alleyways again rang with the shouts of children playing. People bustled around, clearing away months of accumulated dirt, making cabins habitable. The ship was filled with light and a sense of joy and anticipation. The *Anastasis* had truly risen from the grave and we could scrub away the grave clothes! More than that, we all felt that God had resurrected us as well.

Our return to the ship heralded many changes in all our lives. Much to my delight, it meant that my lonely vigils in the hospital were transformed into new and exciting team efforts as I became better acquainted with Doug and Kathryn.

Frequently, we fled the ship together. We huddled close in the crisp spring air perched high on the hillside overlooking the shipyard, avidly discussing our future hopes and dreams. Sometimes we invaded a local coffee house. Here we sat indoors in a large bare room with a dusty floor and close-packed tables jammed tight with men sitting over a thimbleful of fine ground coffee. Our friendship developed rapidly and we were soon as thick as thieves.

The rest of the crew already thought we medics a rather crazy and eccentric department. We scraped, scrubbed and painted, meticulous in every detail, all of us too perfectionistic to do a second rate job. Finishing touches, such as contrasting border trims were exact to a fraction of an inch. If a patient appeared with a cut that required suturing, we operated in overalls, dusting away the paint chips before donning our surgical gloves. Often we resented these interruptions. We were reluctant to leave our construction. By now we seemed more at home with needle guns than with real needles.

The ancient instruments and equipment scattered around the hospital provided a horde of unexpected treasures for the rest of the ship's crew. Some of the ladies already used the old steam sterilizer to cook cakes and puddings. The aroma of these delicious concoctions often drifted down the hospital corridor. They were very disappointed when we decided to remove it from its prime position in the operating room floor.

Discarded needle holders and forceps were much in demand throughout the ship as they had a thousand and one uses from engine room to electrical workshop. Old plaster of Paris makes good patches for worn out pipes, we discovered. Our electronics experts delighted in the valves, switches and other gadgets from obsolete equipment. A true pioneer spirit developed. We never threw anything out until the whole crew had a chance to inspect it. We found much truth in the old adage 'One man's rubbish is another man's treasure'.

Slowly, the hospital was transformed. The dilapidated rooms took on a new glow, reflecting the tremendous effort poured into them. We painted the barren wards pale green with a dark green stripe around the top. Then with great relief, I set aside the needle gun and took to the sewing machine instead. Soon, we proudly displayed green-checked curtains around the newly sanded and painted bunk beds. Not a good choice, I realized later. Not good when I felt seasick! However, at the time it looked wonderful, and was a vast improvement on the rusty bulkheads we started with.

The surgery looked far more inviting. It was pale blue with a dark blue stripe around the ceiling and another stripe around the inside of the surgery light. Our antiquated table was gone, and bolted in its place was a modern hydraulic table with black upholstered covering.

As the hospital expanded our view of the future broadened. Slowly, we started to look ahead, beyond the physical work to the ministry we occasionally caught glimpses of on the horizon. Now, with some of our rooms functional, it was easier to believe that one day our operating room would buzz with activity and a stream of patients would fill the corridors with expectant faces. Maybe there was a possibility that one day we would see deformities healed and lives transformed.

'Where there is no vision, the people perish;' I read in Proverbs 29:18 (KJV). For me, as for the Israelites, vision for the future was an important ingredient of my faith. Without a dream to hold onto my struggles were purposeless and my endeavours meaningless activity.

Thank goodness God gives us images of hope as milestones along the path we tread. I knew it was God's plan to have a hospital on board the *Anastasis* to meet the needs of poor and needy in the Third World. Without that confidence, none of us could have endured the needle gunning and sandpapering that occupied so much of our time. Looking to the future gave us trust for the present. The faithfulness of God in the past was a foundation for trust in all that lay ahead.

Doug, Kathryn and I all tentatively committed our hopes and aspirations to the Lord in prayer. It was a new experience. Before arriving on the *Anastasis*, we all lived in a whirl of activity in which the commotion of the material world easily deadened our spiritual perceptions. The hustle and bustle of our busy lives obscured our ability to see all that God desired. Now, we had little medical work to do and few other distractions. We spent more time in prayer, reading the Bible and just listening for God's direction than we ever did before. Our prayer times were a great excuse to pull us away from the messy business of needle gunning and sanding.

We spent hours discussing, arguing, listening, seeking to translate the intangible visions in our minds into more practical realities. Unfortunately, in the isolation of a shipyard in Greece, there was no one we could call on for help so we really had little idea of what was feasible to establish on a ship. But it did not stop us dreaming and planning and praying, and through the process our faith grew stronger and our belief that God was directing our progress was established.

One scripture verse in particular grabbed our imagination. Isaiah 35:5–7 says

> Then will the eyes of the blind be opened and the ears of the deaf unstopped. Then will the lame leap like a deer, and the mute tongue shout for joy. Water will gush forth in the wilderness and streams in the desert.

We talked constantly about this. Could we perform eye surgery on board? Was it possible to help the lame walk and the deaf speak? We began to think so. This verse seemed like a very tangible promise for the future and one that had both practical and spiritual application. We prayed for the day we would see eyes opened, ears unstopped and the lame leaping for joy both physically and spiritually. We set our eyes on building a hospital for eye surgery, and cleft lip and palate repairs. As well as that, we talked about dental ministry and mobile medical teams to work in impoverished communities. We wanted to perform procedures that would truly open the eyes of the blind and unstop the ears of the deaf.

In this we were joined by the rest of the ship's leaders. Don and Deyon Stephens particularly inspired us with their faith and encouragement. Don believed strongly in the future of the *Anastasis* as a medical ship and had the ability to inspire others with his vision and enthusiasm. Deyon was also a great support and counselled all of us through both our private struggles and our doubts about the ministry. Without them we would probably never have endured the thankless renovation task we had undertaken. They prayed with us and encouraged our endeavours. They listened to our fears and frustrations. Most of all they gave us the hope and the inspiration to continue.

There were other experiences too that contributed to my spiritual growth and development during these last months in Greece. The highlight of these experiences and the one that most helped me in understanding my heritage, was a trip to Kithyra with Ruth, Cheryl and a Greek friend.

This tiny island sitting at the bottom of the Peloponnese peninsula, braced against the full fury of the Mediterranean storms, was my grandfather's birthplace. With its rugged windswept aspect, it was not a place that most people wanted to explore. That didn't deter us. One weekend we borrowed a small Volkswagen car from the ship and boarded the ferry at Pyraeus.

A gale was blowing as we inched our way down the coast along the side of the Peloponnese mountains. Tiny villages clung to the mountainous coastline nestling into the myriad of little bays and inlets. There were few roads, and for their inhabitants, this ferry seemed to be the only contact with the outside world.

One such tiny village had no jetty large enough for the ferry to dock. We anchored at the entrance to the tiny bay and pitched and rolled in the angry white-capped peaks. A small and rather ancient sailing boat slowly and arduously moved toward us out of the mist. Behind it bobbed an even tinier dinghy – surely no one could land in that?

Nothing deterred the local family returning from their monthly shopping spree in Athens. Like the ancient Greek mariners who braved the seas for thousands of years, they were unconcerned by a few crashing waves. The ship's crew and passengers lined the decks offering advice and encouragement. They frantically shouted instructions the moment the boat pulled into the relative calm on the lee side of the ferry. People gesticulated wildly to make themselves understood over the roar of the winds and the waves.

We watched in fascination as the boat was loaded, listening to the unintelligible garble around us. First the TV set disappeared over the side. Then the orange trees and the cavernous shopping bags were juggled down the flimsy rope ladder, into the waiting vessel. The sailing boat sank lower and lower in the water tossing and pitching in the waves. The shouts of the crew and passengers became wilder and more frantic.

By now the boat was so heavily laden, the foam-flecked waves sloshed constantly over the sides. We were sure nothing else could be loaded. But no, we were wrong! With renewed shouts of enthusiastic advice from the crew, the family too, began to disembark. First came grandma, hesitant but determined as she clutched at her billowing long black dress and tightly secured headscarf. Then grandpa scurried down the ladder with an expression of unconcerned disdain. Mum came next, in her high-heeled shoes and Sunday go-to-church outfit. Finally dad and the three children clambered down into the tiny boat.

The vessel sank lower and lower in the water and the occupants huddled together as protection against the sea spray. We were sure the boat would sink the moment it left the relative calm by the ferry. The angry waves bared their white teeth, waiting hungrily to devour their unexpected meal.

We watched in fascination as the vessel began its tortuous journey homeward, egged on by the exultant cries of the watching crowd. It caught the full force of the wind as it left the ferry's sheltering side and staggered into the embrace of the storm edging slowly toward the jetty. Much to our relief it docked without mishap. The occupants apparently unconcerned by their treacherous journey, gazed back at us triumphantly. The drama was over, at least for the moment.

As our ferry approached the island of Kithyra we realized that more fun and games lay in store. The gathering dusk obscured most of our view but a few lights twinkling weakly on the shore revealed a picture we would rather not face. A small wharf protruded from the tiny cove around which the township of Kithyra was built. It had little protection from the sea and the waves, now lashed to a wild frenzy by the storm, crashed relentlessly against the adjacent sea wall.

The ferry gingerly manoeuvred alongside, and through the dim grey light and misty sea spray we could vaguely discern a large building. It was at right angles to the car ramp and loomed ominously close, only twenty-five feet beyond the end of the jetty. We watched anxiously as the ship's ramp slid crazily back and forth, only too well aware that it was our only exit route. One minute it was securely against the roadway, the next it was hanging precariously over the edge of the sea wall. A misplaced step would send us crashing into the boiling inferno beneath us.

The Greeks are born with a love of drama in their veins and this situation suited them perfectly. The crew instantly came to life, like actors in a play. The whole world was their stage and the howling wind and roaring seas combined to produce a wonderful bizarre orchestral accompaniment.

The boatswain balanced himself precariously on the wildly swaying car ramp in anticipation of our departure – he was obviously the conductor. The wind whipped around him, tossing the foaming waves viciously against the sea wall beside him. Sea spray dripped from his black hair and down his bright yellow raincoat. The rest of the crew fussed around our little car like protective hens around their chickens. We felt they were ready, if need be, to throw our vehicle bodily from the ferry should our driving skills fail to come up to scratch.

The boatswain gestured dramatically toward our little Volkswagen, waving us forward to what looked like certain disaster. By unanimous consent, Ruth was driving. She learned to drive in Paris and we thought she possessed all the manoeuvring skills of a professional race car driver. The rest of us sat nervously on the edge of our seats, praying fervently. Ruth revved the motor loudly and took a firm and determined hold on the steering wheel. 'Ella, Ella (Come, come)' the boatswain shouted as we hesitated briefly and our little Volkswagen jerked forward a few feet. Then suddenly it was 'Ompa, ompa (Stop, stop)' as the ship's movement pushed the ramp out over the open sea and Ruth slammed on the brakes as a gaping hole opened between us and the wharf's edge. Anxiously, we waited for the next wave to hurl the ferry back against the dock. People crowded around us, shouting instructions, encouraging our progress. The ship groaned with the effort adding its voice to the growing cacophony of sound. Then suddenly our opportunity arrived. The boatswain, the crew, and the waiting passengers screamed 'Ella, ella' in unison, Ruth accelerated suddenly and the car shot off the vessel like a bullet out of a gun. We careered wildly across the wet ramp as the ferry began its slow retreat, skidded onto the island and slammed on the brakes just in time to avoid the building. Ruth pulled frantically on the wheel and we slid gracefully round the corner away from the danger. We cheered with relief, thankful to be safe and sound on the island.

After such an auspicious arrival our sojourn on Kithyra was something of an anticlimax. We discovered the dilapidated village of Arondothica, soon dubbed 'Aroneyville' by Cheryl and even managed to locate the derelict pile of rubble which marked my forebear's house. It was all very forlorn. Tiny white houses clung to the hillsides like limpets grimly holding their own against the ferocious winds that continually battered the island. Windswept, bleak and almost deserted, the village appeared a sad reminder of a bygone age.

Most of the inhabitants had migrated to Australia. Only a few of the elderly people remained to continue the battle. They were stocky, hardy individuals with pale blue eyes and black hair like my relatives back home. I was proud that their blood flowed in my veins. That fierce pride which dominated the world thousands of years ago was still there, coupled with a stubborn endurance and tenacity necessary to survive in such conditions. Perhaps that explained in part my persistence during those long hard months of rehabilitation on the ship.

During the Second World War these people provided one of the few escape routes for British soldiers fleeing the German advance. Today they still refuse to give in to the enemies that surround them. The advance of a civilization which has sent their children sweeping around the world to more congenial settings could not rob them of the freedoms of this island which has been theirs for countless generations. A deep admiration welled up from within. This island too was part of my heritage and I prayed that the tenacity and endurance which I saw there had also passed down through the ages to me and my family.

In view of this adventure and the assortment of learning opportunities I experienced, it was with very mixed feelings that I finally said goodbye to Greece, after a stay of over eighteen months. The *Anastasis* itself had been there for three years of long and arduous work.

Our departure was a triumphant exit orchestrated in such a way that it was impossible for us not to believe God was in our midst. I was overawed by the evidence of his concern for minute details and by the incredible way he wove together the parts of a very complex tapestry into a beautiful design.

For months the crew waited impatiently to sail. We constantly joked about our regular spurts of activity designed to get the ship under way. We laughed a lot, but underneath our laughter and spoofs was a gnawing doubt that maybe the local people were right and the harbour of Elevsis could still be both our birthplace and our grave. Even our miraculous exit from the graveyard did not sustain us for long.

Finally however the engines purred into life and the ship was ready to sail, and miracle of miracles, the tanks were full of fuel. What an occasion that had been. We had danced round the decks late at night singing and rejoicing as the fuel barge came alongside. We watched in joyful anticipation as the hoses were hooked up and the black life giving liquid was pumped aboard. David Bogenrieff was out with his trumpet playing triumphant songs of praise to God. Our tanks went from totally empty to full and overflowing in one short night and that to us was a miracle.

For weeks beforehand we were so short of fuel that the generators only operated a couple of hours a day. There was no hot water, it was too expensive to heat the boiler and we all took bucket baths. Ruth and Cheryl and I worked out a marvellous routine to heat maximum hot water in minimum time. First we heated a kettle-full for a shower, then we made a pot of tea, then finally we filled our thermos flasks for the evening. And if it was cold, the last kettle-full of water went into my hot-water bottle. Without it, I would not survive the night.

Every couple of days the engine crew rolled a couple of drums down to the local service station and filled them with diesel. Then the motormen stood down in the engine room, hour after dreary hour, stirring the diesel and sludge together. Sometimes the resulting mixture was too thick and the generator whined and groaned in protest. The lights dimmed warningly or occasionally went out completely leaving us in the pitch black. We were all attuned to changes in tone from the generators anticipating the sounds that meant another breakdown. At times I think it was only our prayers that kept the fuel moving.

Now our tanks were full and we were anxious to be out of Greece. With great anticipation we hoisted the 'Blue Peter' – the flag that means a ship is due to sail within twenty-four hours. We also festooned the rest of the ship with colourful signal flags. Most of us hardly slept, we were so excited. But the days dragged on. One, two, three . . . the banks were on strike and we couldn't get our money . . . the supplies for the sail hadn't arrived. The final details seemed to go so slowly and those days passed at a snail's pace.

At last the tugs drew alongside ready to pull us out of our berth. The sun shone brilliantly and the blue sky beamed upon us. Heaven seemed to join our anticipation and rejoicing. We were all on deck cheering and shouting as the crew threw off the ropes and cast us free. We watched excitedly as the ship inched its way out of the berth. Even then Greece seemed determined to hold onto us. Our anchor chain tangled itself with those of the adjacent ships and it took hours to shake it free. We lifted the mess of chains high and crashed them to the bottom of the sea again hoping the impact would release us. We repeated the manoeuvre time and again and still they hung on. Finally one anchor was free and then the other rose with pieces of broken chain attached like tentacles to its prongs. At last, we were released from our imprisonment and the *Anastasis* headed out past Pyraeus and into the open sea.

Chapter 5

A HOSPITAL IS BORN

Where there is no vision the people perish
                                        Prov 29:18 (KJV)

We pulled up anchor exactly three years after the ship's arrival in Greece. It was July 7th, 1982, the seventh day of the seventh month. Obviously perfect timing from God's perspective. The last vestiges of the grave were thrown off and we were free at last. Triumphantly we sailed out of Pyraeus Harbour, through the Mediterranean Sea and across the Atlantic Ocean toward the Panama Canal, the Pacific Ocean and Los Angeles.

Unfortunately, our exuberance at leaving the place of our imprisonment died rapidly. We sailed out of Pyraeus into a vicious storm that sorely tested our rather shaky sealegs. Most of us were seasoned landlubbers and soon discovered we were not very seaworthy at all.

At first it was amusing. We watched Esther, one of the children who had just learned to walk, try to balance herself on the heaving deck. She staggered forward and the deck came up to meet her. She moved again and there was no deck at all beneath her feet. She fell backwards onto her well-padded bottom and sat there with a puzzled expression on her face. Yesterday her balance was perfect. We laughed and adopting the sailor's wide-based swaggering gait we left her to her struggles. We blithely traipsed down to the kitchen to receive our ration of empty jam containers. They were gallon-sized plastic pots with handles, and the thoughtful galley staff had saved them in case we were seasick. Of course none of us thought we would need them.

'Anti seasickness pills are being distributed in the hospital,' we announced, as the wind whipped up the waves around us. 'Come to the aft deck for your sea sickness pills' we corrected, half-an-hour later as the medical staff ventured out into the fresh air. By now, the green of my face matched the green of my blouse and I was trying valiantly to stop the upheaval of my insides. 'Don't bother about coming to me for your seasickness medicine. The doctor is sicker than you are,' I felt like saying a little later as I gave up the unequal struggle and retired to my bunk. My worst fears were realized. Less than twenty-four hours at sea and I was already violently ill. Why on earth had I come to work on a ship?

Fortunately, our discomfort was short-lived and the storm soon abated. The angry white peaks flattened to smooth, glass-like seas that sparkled beneath a brilliant blue sky. Fair weather and a following wind blessed our passage. Schools of playful dolphins often cavorted exuberantly alongside the ship. We hung over the bow to watch their antics. We played games out on the aft deck, pulling out the old shuttle board sets and deck chairs hidden in the holds for years. The deck crew filled the swimming pool for the first time and we relaxed in it late at night watching the brilliantly shining stars in the jet black night. We pretended we were on a luxurious vacation cruise. For someone as prone to seasickness as I am, it seemed like a miracle and I relished every minute of it.

A glorious night sail through the Panama canal provided the grand finale to a wonderful twenty-eight day cruise. It was dinner time when the locks that raised us up to the canal came in sight. We bolted our food and hurried back on deck. None of us wanted to miss a moment of the spectacle. Wire ropes secured the ship fore and aft. Small mechanical powerhouses, called donkeys, hurried along on railway tracks beside the ship with the steel ropes firmly in their grasp. They quickly manoeuvred us into position inside the lock.

We peered inquisitively over the side as the water level rose, watching in fascination as the *Anastasis* moved higher and higher. In the adjacent lock, an enormous cargo vessel sank slowly in the opposite direction, down to the Atlantic. Its huge bulk dwarfed the *Anastasis*. It looked as though it had been crammed into the small space with a shoe horn. Ahead of us, a small sailing boat swayed to and fro in its own enormous compartment . . . it had plenty of room to manoeuvre.

We passed through one lock, then another and then another slowly moving higher, until we emerged into the canal itself. By now it was dusk and a warm pink glow hung over the thick tropical forests. Tangled jungle, tightly packed with tall trees and choking vines, loomed out of the dark on both sides. Bright flashes of red and green and blue marked the passing of exotic birds, their shrill calls interspersed with the grunts and groans of strange animals that beckoned with their promise of the unknown. The *Anastasis* glided eerily along the narrow channel like a gigantic car on a busy, well lit highway. The traffic stretched ahead and behind, thin grey lines in the tropical twilight, two constant streams from Atlantic to Pacific oceans. None of us could sleep we were so entranced by the incredible sight.

Six hours later we entered another set of locks to bring us down into the Pacific – only two this time. They beckoned us on into this new ocean for the last few days of our cruise. It was as brilliant and as calm as the Atlantic had been. What a blessing this first cruise was. It was a special gift from God, a surprise present that seemed like a beautiful reward for all the struggles and sacrifices of the previous years.

None of this, however, prepared us for our welcome in Los Angeles. It was a hot, dry July day. A searing wind whipped up the coal dust from an adjacent mound and deposited it on the huge crowd of over 2000 exultant well-wishers waiting expectantly at Pier 53 as we sailed in. Nothing dampened their enthusiasm. Many of these people had been praying for the *Anastasis* and its crew for years. Others had only just heard about this Christian ship that was called to serve the nations. All came to rejoice with us as our ministry was launched.

Yet our arrival was also tinged with sadness. The strains of 'Holy Holy Holy', sung by Keith Green, wafted across the water as we were manoeuvred into our berth. It was a very nostalgic moment. The music was taped. It was only a week since Keith's death in a plane crash. He was meant to be part of the arrival ceremony. His wife, Melody, was there to greet us instead.

The crowd cheered and shouted as we threw out our ropes and secured the ship. The tugs gently nudged us into place. Doug, Kathryn and I stood on the promenade deck waving frantically to familiar faces in the crowd. Cheryl Robertson and David Cowie were there. They had flown ahead to prepare for the ship's arrival. David Cowie's mother was there, too. I knew her from New Zealand and was eagerly anticipating seeing her again. Doug and Kathryn's friends waved at us – I was looking forward to meeting them. We could hardly wait to get ashore and show off all we had accomplished in the last few years. We were dressed to impress too and for the first time we were wearing our smart new white uniforms complete with epaulettes and medical insignias. We wanted this first impression to be a good one.

The crowd swarmed over the dock, hovering around the gangway like bees around a honey pot. They waited anxiously for the signal to come aboard. Unfortunately the LA Fire Brigade had other ideas. Within moments of our arrival the first hitches to our well laid plans occurred. Our gangway was too small to deal with the crowds we were expecting and the fire department insisted another larger one be installed to direct people straight onto the aft deck. An enormous contraption, something like an ungainly metal grandstand on wheels awaited our arrival. It was five storeys high and twenty feet long. Our welders stood poised ready for action – their job to bolt it into position and dismantle the ship's railing. The crowds waited patiently in anticipation.

The new gangway inched closer and closer across the dock, until it rested against the hull. Then it heaved and twisted like a bucking bronco as the swell grabbed the ship and pushed it hard against the wharf. The giant tyres inserted between the ship's side and the wharf to cushion our impact squealed like outraged pigs as we crunched against them. Another wave rushed up the narrow inlet sucking the ship along the wharf. The protesting gangway was dragged with it. Hurriedly the deck crew pushed it away. Our crowds would just have to wait until another more acceptable gangway could be built. So much for that first good impression.

Fortunately this inauspicious beginning did not seem to deter our well-wishers. Over the next few months, we were deluged with people. Friends, families, church parties and tourists all came to see the refurbished *Anastasis*. They swarmed on board at all hours expecting tours, asking questions or participating in work parties. Everyone was eager to find out more about our mission. Many simply came to look and, to their own surprise, stayed to help. Some even decided to sign up as crew members. Never again would we feel alone, deserted in a Greek backwash where nothing happened.

The ship captured the imagination of many who visited. Each day of our five month sojourn in Los Angeles brought new helpers, blessing us with their knowledge and expertise. Architects, carpenters, medical advisers, as well as doctors and dentists all contributed their thoughts and ideas. In the hospital, they admired our checked curtains and freshly painted bunks. They gasped in horror at the stories of hardship we told and listened expectantly to our ideas for the bare and empty rooms we showed them. Some shook their heads in disbelief at the seemingly preposterous plans we envisioned for the future of this ship-based hospital.

Sometimes we groaned under the weight of the constant attention and enthusiasm. I found it particularly hard to force a smile when a visitor interrupted my meal and it was even harder to welcome an out of town guest who arrived late at night, eager to be shown round the vessel. My legs ached from the unexpected exercise as each tour required a climb up and down eight steep staircases as we moved from bridge to engine room and back to reception.

Work parties invaded the hospital. They uprooted bunk beds, stripped bulkheads, sorted drugs. They sanded, painted and made cabinets. The hospital changed literally in front of our eyes. With the help of our army of volunteers we accomplished far more in those five months than in the previous two years, and much to our delight we no longer wielded the needle guns or paint brushes ourselves.

A medical laboratory took shape out of what had been two tiny bunk rooms. The dust flew as a church singles group attacked the area with hammers and saws one Saturday morning. These rooms hadn't been entered for years. The mattresses were old and mouldy. The dust was inches thick. But that enthusiastic church group didn't care. With great delight they cut out the wall and uprooted the bunks from their metal sockets. Then they followed up with sanders and paint brushes. A bright new room emerged.

Then came the real challenge – the cabinets. Nothing in those rooms was symmetrical, nothing predictable. Decks and bulkheads sloped at odd angles and unexpected protrusions made carpentry a nightmare. Every cupboard, bench and bookcase had to be individually designed and crafted. No two units were ever the same. Amazingly, highly-skilled craftsmen, the best quality materials, first-class equipment were all provided. A beautiful new lab developed before our eyes.

A dental unit also arrived on board provided by three young dentists. They were some of those meal-time visitors I wanted to throw overboard. There was Terry, a tall intense young man with black curly hair and a visionary gleam in his eyes. With him were Jim, suave and sophisticated with his immaculate grooming and designer clothing and Mike who looked as though he could do with a good exercise routine. They peered into every nook and cranny in the ship and stayed until midnight enthusiastically discussing their plans for dental ministry. We waved them good-bye, our bodies exhausted but our spirits ignited with a new vision.

Then a friendly architect appeared. He listened attentively to our dreams and contributed blueprints and sketches to help us focus. He even drew seagulls in the portholes for authenticity.

Almost daily we headed to Don Stephen's office with new ideas and demands for space. His eyes sparkled behind his glasses as he listened enthusiastically to our plans. 'The medical lab is too small,' we explained one day. 'We can't manage without an X-ray,' we cried the next. 'And what about a dental unit and dental lab?' we demanded excitedly. 'More space for patients,' was our next desperate cry. Don always greeted us with an encouraging grin. He listened patiently to our requests, diplomatically curbing our enthusiasm when it looked as though we would soon take over the whole ship.

We abounded in inexperience and ignorance regarding hospital construction, yet miraculously it was being built. Those insubstantial dreams we formulated back in Greece were taking on form. The words from Is 35:5-6 came back to my mind. I started to believe that with God's guidance and our hard work we would one day see 'the eyes of the blind opened and the ears of the deaf unstopped.' I longed for the day we would help 'the lame leap like a deer and the mute tongue shout for joy.' These words were like a signpost, building our confidence, encouraging our faith, inspiring our hope for the future.

In fact, we could almost visualize the hospital in full operation before our very eyes. Here was a little boy in Mexico having a cleft lip repaired, a blind granny in Togo having her sight restored and a young man in Angola using a new prosthetic limb. We could almost imagine ourselves involved with our God, healing, touching, loving, bringing new life in the name of our Lord Jesus Christ.

Equipment and supplies arrived too, at all hours of the day and night and from all over the country. Sometimes we didn't know who had donated them. To us it was an even more substantial confirmation of our plans, though at times it was difficult to remain grateful.

'Not another load!' I exclaimed, gritting my teeth as another large truck drove onto the dock. I tried desperately to engender some enthusiasm for the bandages and syringes being disgorged from its depths. The truck came from Florida and we didn't even know who had sent it. The harassed deck crew, bewildered and frustrated by these disruptions to their routines laboured diligently to assist us.

Cartons littered the hospital, trying our patience, creating chaos around us. Our unfinished rooms started to look like a junkyard before an auction. Boxes oozed into the passageways. No sooner was one load unpacked and disposed of than another appeared to take its place. We constructed shelves in one of the cargo holds. They soon bulged with boxes as well. We had no idea what some of them contained. Such abundant provision was poured upon us that it was many months before everything was sorted and properly stored.

In spite of this provision, Doug and I still struggled to believe God would provide all the expensive equipment we needed. Understanding our doubts and struggles more intimately than we understood them ourselves, God took great pains to prove his faithfulness. Often we were caught completely unawares by the unexpected answers.

We desperately needed an X-ray machine, not an ordinary machine, but one that would fit into a tiny 8ft x 8ft room with an even smaller washroom for developing. We gathered a stack of leaflets on possible units, but none of them seemed viable. They were all too expensive, or too big, or too complicated to run. And all of them seemed to take too much power. We would drain half the ship's AC power supply each time we took an X-ray. It just didn't seem feasible.

However, God had other plans. One day a dark haired young man detached himself from the tour group wending its way through the ship. He poked his nose into the hospital and confronted us with a question. 'Do you need an X-ray machine? My company would like to donate one to you.' We listened in stunned amazement as he told his story. He worked for an X-ray firm owned by Christians. His company wanted to tithe from their profits to the *Anastasis*. They wanted to give us an X-ray machine, hand-picked to meet our needs. Our visitor also offered to install it and show us how to operate it.

We were both delighted and amazed. Such unex-pected provision took our breath away. God's faith-fulness constantly astounded us. Even when our faith was not strong enough to pray or even believe. Slowly God was building up our confidence in his ability and willingness to provide all that we needed, even when we were afraid to ask.

Work in the hospital was still gruelling. The moun-tain of work sent out its tentacles seemingly deter-mined to devour us. It plucked away our leisure time and entangled us in a web of work the likes of which we had never seen before. Often we laboured throughout the evening, sacrificing our days off too in order to keep ahead of deadlines. The boundaries between work and pleasure became blurred and even our fun revolved around our growing hospital. Fortunately there were some entertaining moments to lighten our burdens. They helped defuse our grow-ing stresses and breathe fresh life into us. Many of these entertaining moments were provided by Doug and his love of fishing.

Fish abounded in the LA harbour, and Doug soon had fishing lines protruding from every hospital porthole. Bait added its distinctive odour to the drugs in our refrigerator, and the delicate aroma of fish per-vaded our surroundings. The crew was highly amused by our antics. Their constant question was not 'How many patients have you seen today?' but 'Are the fish biting? How many have you caught?'

The fish always managed to bite at the most inopportune moments. One morning I was holding crew clinic when the familiar whirring sound attracted my attention. My patient was a new crew member, unconversant with the eccentricities of the *Anastasis* medical staff. She was seriously describing her symptoms to me when I suddenly jumped up and raced to the door. 'There's a fish on the line,' I yelled down the corridor. My horrified patient was convinced that I had cracked under the strain and I was obviously no longer capable of rational conversation.

Doug dashed into the room and stuck his head out of the porthole. The rest of the medical staff were close on his heels. They all wanted to be a part of the action. My patient watched with growing confusion and anxiety as one nurse grabbed a net and raced down to the deck below to help with the delicate operation. Soon we were all hanging through the portholes holding our breath as Doug manoeuvred his wriggling load out of the water and up the side of the ship. There was a ten foot drop from the porthole to the ocean and we had lost a fish there just a couple of days ago. But this one was firmly attached. The nurse below us secured it in the net and Doug inched it up to the hospital. Soon a 4 lb steelhead lay gasping its life out on the hospital floor. My patient backed towards the door and darted for her cabin. We tried to explain, but I don't think she ever really trusted us with her care again. After all, she had come to consult a doctor not to participate in a fishing tournament.

On another occasion we were showing the president and staff of a large pharmaceutical company around, when that well-known whirr accosted our ears. We were dressed in our immaculate new white uniforms to create a good impression but the fish soon changed that. Dignity, pomp and ceremony all went by the board and our distinguished guests were soon all hanging out of the portholes. They were fishing enthusiasts too and the ensuing battle with the landing of a good sized steelhead was, I think, the highlight of their visit. I am sure they never forgot the crew of this Mercy Ship for whom anything could happen and the unexpected was commonplace.

We made some wonderful friends during our five month stay in Los Angeles. Dr Will Davies and his wife Nadine, for example, attended a reception for medical personnel and never seemed to leave. Will, a burns specialist from Torrance, California, was not your typical doctor. He looked like a big shaggy dog with tight curly hair and overalls. He wandered from the engine room to the bridge inquisitively asking questions and ferreting out information. He brought us sandpaper and paint, vacuum cleaners and hammers from home. He raided the storage room of Torrance Memorial Hospital and discovered medical equipment and supplies.

Nadine Davies was a slender wiry woman with boundless energy and enthusiasm. She organized work parties and spent arduous hours with her friends surrounded by a sea of boxes. They popped pills out of small sample packs and consolidated them into large jars. Their efforts often reduced a large box to a single small container.

A couple of days before the ship left Los Angeles, Will appeared yet again with an unexpected gift. This time he clutched a desk-top computer under his arm.

He was an ardent computer junkie and thought that I should be too. All we had time for was one quick five minute lesson and then the ship was pulling up anchor and heading south for Guatemala and New Zealand. I was left with yet another challenge to add to my growing list.

As we pulled out from the dock, I sadly waved goodbye to Doug and Kathryn who were staying in the US for the birth of their first child. I thought of the four lonely months that lay ahead. We had become a very close-knit team in that last year and it seemed hard to believe that anyone else could fill the gap they left. I doubted my ability to carry the vision alone.

Once again God came to the rescue. Firstly, through the strength and support of the rest of the community on board. Secondly, through the provision of Chris MacLean, a nurse consultant who had just returned to California from Israel and Saudi Arabia.

Chris was tiny. She stood five foot nothing in her stockinged feet and looked as though the next puff of wind would blow her overboard. It was hard to believe she had already spent many years working successfully under difficult conditions in the Third World. Now she was willing to give it a go on board the *Anastasis*. I couldn't believe my good luck.

Chris and I already knew we had much in common. We are both half Greek and our common heritage gave us a bond which helped to quickly develop a good working relationship. Fortunately for me too, there was one thing we didn't have in common – Chris does not get seasick easily, so I quickly elected her to attend the patients when we sailed.

The waves crashed remorselessly against the ship as we ploughed our way south from Los Angeles to

Champerico, Guatemala. We were heading into another storm. It seemed this was the way we always initiated our new recruits. Once again, we were weltering in the misery of seasickness. It robbed us, at least temporarily, of the joy of sailing on our first mission of mercy.

The decks pitched and rolled as I lurched down the corridor to attend a patient in need. A green tinge to my complexion and a bucket under my arm proclaimed that I too was feeling the effects of the weather . . . again!

'Why do I get myself into such situations?' I fumed self-pityingly. My tendency to succumb to the least degree of motion was already a well-used joke on board. Some of the crew even phoned down to the hospital to check on my state, surmising that if I was up and functional that they should be too. Why intentionally put myself through days of misery? There must be an easier way to serve the Lord.

I did not have far to look, however, for the answer. Our holds contained hundreds of thousands of dollars worth of cargo for refugee relief in Guatemala. Food, clothes, medicine and building supplies were packaged and ready to go. It was but a drop in the bucket in comparison to their needs, but to us was a symbol of all that was to come. We believed it represented the first fruits of a ministry that would one day help many around the world. To bring comfort and practical assistance to the destitute and the homeless was worth even the agonies of seasickness.

When the coast of Guatemala appeared on the horizon, we all breathed a sigh of relief. Now at last we would find a haven, a rest from the rolling and pitching that had made us so miserable. At least that was what this seasick doctor thought.

As the ship drew closer, however, we realized that no large and bustling port awaited our arrival. Champerico was a small town with minimal facilities. From the ship, all we could see was an old jetty jutting out into the sea from a seemingly endless shoreline.

The *Anastasis* anchored a quarter of a mile off shore, rolling constantly in the unpleasant swell. Large steel barges battered through the still angry seas to meet us. With horror I realized that this was our only way to go ashore. Not only would they unload our cargo, but our passengers as well.

With a bone crushing jolt which reverberated throughout the ship, the first barge drew alongside. The wooden ladder shattered into toothpicks but a rope ladder quickly replaced it. I stuck my head out through the hospital porthole and watched in horror as people began to disembark. I waited anxiously for one of them to be crunched against the side too. I prayed frantically, or was it a plea? I didn't want to deal with the injuries my vivid imagination conjured up.

Fortunately my fears were unfounded. The barge handlers caught each descending passenger with amazing finesse, synchronizing their movements with the pitching rolling vessels. Everyone landed without a single scratch. I heaved a sigh of relief.

By the next day I too was ready to brave this new experience and longed to escape the constant nausea and dizziness. I staggered down the ladder with Chris MacLean and a group of friends and exuberantly headed towards the land unaware that this was only stage one in the adventurous saga necessary to deliver us to Champerico.

The jetty itself stood forty or fifty feet above the water level. Old and dilapidated after many years of service it was obviously much in need of repair. Rotting boards left gaps like giant cavities through which the sunlight gleamed with remorseless tropical intensity. A pungent odour of decaying sugar cane and banana palms permeated the area. To our uninitiated eyes there was no apparent means of reaching the platform above. Only the old cargo nets remained, their machinery, rusty and noisy, looking like some relic from a bygone age.

We watched nervously, as with much creaking and groaning the cargo nets were lowered into the boat. This was our means of ascent. Hesitantly six of us stepped inside and clung grimly to the old and smelly ropes around us. Swallowing our fear, we shut our eyes and prayed fervently. The net swung upward with a jolt and moved hesitantly toward the pier. With a final groan and another jolt, it deposited its pale faced cargo safe and sound at the top of that terrible ascent. We felt we could identify with the missionaries of old who had faced many unknown dangers as they shared the gospel in unevangelized lands.

That night, we attended a church service held by local evangelical Christians. Cheryl, who spoke fluent Spanish, translated for us. She had braved an extremely rough crossing from the ship that afternoon to join us. 'There is another storm brewing,' she informed us as she strode along the dock in her bright red culottes and white blouse. 'We won't be able to return to the ship tonight.' We were stranded but it didn't detract from our enjoyment of that special evening.

The Guatemalans crowded into a small stuffy room, excited to join in worship with their sisters and brothers from other nations. They strummed their guitars with a grace and vigour that brought new life to the songs and music. They sang with rich deep voices that communicated their exuberant faith and love for God.

Afterwards, our new Christian friends helped us find an inexpensive hotel for the night. They guided us towards what looked like a derelict hovel which was dank and dark with water dripping down the walls. We were ushered into two rooms, one for the men and one for the women. We surveyed the furniture in dismay. The beds were only about five feet long, and made for small Guatemalans. There were no blankets or sheets and we would have to sleep with two people squashed together in each bed. We were so exhausted after our busy day we were more than ready to share.

The night grew cold and we shivered against each other, wrapping our ineffectual summer garments around us. Some of us had eaten from street vendors during the day and developed diarrhoea. At least our frequent trips to the dirty smelly toilet at the end of the corridor helped keep us warm.

This was my very first exposure to a developing nation. My mind reeled with new and uncomfortable impressions. As we wandered around Champerico and spent the night in that atrocious hotel, I was shocked by what I saw. Small wooden shacks lined the dusty road. A single room often housed a family of eight or ten. Children in dirty rags and bare feet played amongst the pigs that roamed freely through the villages. Many of the youngsters had pot bellies and reddish hair, the obvious signs of malnutrition. The local doctor appeared as we approached and pleaded for help. The villagers could not afford the medications they required to treat their illnesses. He hoped we could help him fight the unending war against poverty and disease.

Even on board the ship we were inundated with pleas for help. One of the local port officials brought his entire family. His children too were malnourished and listless, having ear infections and worm infestations. We had so little to give but fossicked through our supplies for antibiotics and worm medicine. My heart ached. I longed more than ever for the day we would be fully operational, able to give from our abundance to the desperate needs we encountered.

And then came the church service. These same seemingly impoverished people worshipped God with an exuberance I had rarely experienced in Western churches. I was so confused. How did the teachings of blessing and prosperity I grew up with fit into this environment? Did God promise health and wholeness for these people too or were material blessings just for those of us from the First World?

As we sailed out of Champerico, I grappled with my unsettled thoughts. The poverty, the pain and the heartache I had glimpsed would never be forgotten. Nor would the exuberance and courage of those Guatemalan Christians who faced such unbelievable challenges to their lives. It rocked me to the core of my being. It was as though God had once again taken up his needle gun and started scraping away. at my life. Unfortunately, the further we moved physically from the poverty of that little town, the further the impact receded from my thoughts. With relief, I pushed my uneasy conscience to the back of my mind.

Chapter 6

RETURN TO THE LAND OF THE LONG WHITE CLOUD

Those who sow in tears will reap with songs of joy. He who goes out weeping, carrying seed to sow, will return with songs of joy, carrying sheaves with him.

Ps 126:5,6

The cultured English voice of the BBC announcer intoned the cricket scores over the radio. It was our first indication that we were approaching New Zealand. After two weeks at sea, with only a brief stop in Tahiti to take on fresh water, we were all looking forward to sighting land and hung over the bow watching the smudge on the horizon take shape.

I could hardly believe my good fortune. It is not often a missionary has a chance to bring their mission station home. Yet here I was sailing into the land that had been my home for five years with my whole ministry and a 500 ft ship in tow. I didn't have slides or photos, I had the real thing. I was looking forward to seeing my friends and colleagues again. I wanted to share my visions and dreams for the future as well as my newly developed skills at needle gunning. I hoped to enlist their help to bring the medical ministry on the *Anastasis* fully into being.

We started our New Zealand tour in beautiful

sunny summer weather at the beginning of February. Our first port of call was the tiny, sleepy township of Opua. It nestles in a tiny cove beside the breathtaking turquoise waters of Bay of Plenty, near the northern tip of the two islands. Around us, sheep and cattle grazed on swards of green among the hills patched with remnants of forest and scrub. Thousands of visitors gathered here each year for Waitangi Day, commemorating the taking of New Zealand as a British colony in 1840. We relished the privilege of being part of these celebrations. The entrance of a long narrow Maori war canoe with its high intricately carved prow, provided the highlight for our visit. It glided majestically ashore powered by dozens of brown skinned warriors with bare glistening chests and traditional Maori dress.

From there, we gathered momentum, sailing down the coast to Whangerei, Auckland, Tauranga, Hawkes Bay, Gisborne and Wellington then on to the South Island. The crowds of visitors grew as TV and newspaper stories regarding the mission of the *Anastasis* caught the imagination of the New Zealand people.

Tauranga, with the dominating presence of the flat-topped cone of Mount Maunganui looming over it, was home port for our chief engineer, John Brignall. The township was an unusual combination of industrial port and holiday beach resort. For us, it was a particularly busy stay and we were were caught unawares by the enormous crowds. On some days up to 2000 people visited the ship.

On our first Saturday in port, the ship hummed with activity. The long queues waiting patiently for tours, stood three deep beside the ship, winding around the wharf like a gigantic centipede drowsing in the sun. On top of that, John's daughter, Alison was getting married and we prepared a wedding reception for her and her husband on the aft deck. The wedding party and guests wended their way through the waiting crowds who gawked admiringly at this unexpected addition to their tour.

We hardly had time to draw breath from the afternoon's activities, before hundreds of exuberant young people gathered for the evening. A live band set up stage against the ship's hull and soon the sound of electric guitars and rhythmic drumbeats reverberated through the hull. Then the hordes of teenagers stampeded on board with excited shouts and wild screams. Ruth and Cheryl, who were responsible for such events, were almost overwhelmed by the unexpected onslaught. They heroically recruited volunteers from all departments to deal with their crisis.

In Nelson, at the top of the South Island, a retired dentist came to visit for a quick tour and ended up joining the *Anastasis* for the rest of our New Zealand trip. Our dental room was unusable and the dental unit still packed in the manufacturer's boxes, but he was undeterred. Like most New Zealanders, he was a born fix-it man. He cleared a space in the chaos of our partly constructed conference room and put together the giant dental jigsaw puzzle. First he assembled the dental chair, then the suction unit and the drills. Soon we had a functioning dental unit proudly displayed.

Over the next few weeks this innovative dentist examined patients and drilled teeth surrounded by a wallow of boxes. Local volunteers unpacked and sorted around him. His background music was the sound of construction workers on the far side of the room. In his spare time he worked on the dental room itself, and by the end of the trip had triumphantly installed himself in this newly completed room.

Medical supplies continued to arrive as well. When we arrived in New Zealand I sent a letter to every pharmaceutical company in the country. It was my first fumbling effort at using that new computer for more than a short letter and I was very proud of the results. Much to our surprise many of the companies responded enthusiastically. In Wellington, ICI Chemicals received a copy of our needs list. Their representative marked off every item the company manufactured and before our departure delivered a huge shipment of supplies, apologizing profusely for the items they were unable to provide. In every port, packages arrived by mail or courier. Others were hand delivered by local doctors or pharmaceutical representatives. It was like Christmas, and the New Zealanders' generosity and enthusiasm overwhelmed us. Now we had all the anti-malarials we needed for the South Pacific Islands and an abundance of antibiotics for our own needs and for outreach amongst the poor as well. This time it looked as though we would not have to say 'no' to the people we came to serve.

When the *Anastasis* berthed in Lyttleton, the port of Christchurch, I felt like a returning heroine. Tucked between the wharves and the steep rim of an extinct volcanic crater, Lyttleton township has all the salty atmosphere of an old maritime centre. However for most of us, there wasn't time to enjoy the picturesque harbour. Friends and well-wishers wended their way from Christchurch, my home for five years, over the winding road that crossed the rim of that crater, and descended on the ship like a flock of chirping birds. They dragged me up and down those eight flights of stairs until my legs ached from the unaccustomed exercise. They listened to my stories of needle gunning and seasickness over and over again until I could have repeated them in my sleep. They ushered me into innumerable receptions and banquets for religious, civic and medical groups. I smiled and smiled at the blur of faces until my muscles felt fixed in position. I ate endless meals of turkey and mashed potatoes – sometimes twice a day. By the time we left I thought I probably looked like a turkey.

I spoke at churches and medical meetings. I did TV and radio interviews. On several occasions I picked up the phone and found myself engaged in a live interview. It was scary, and made me very nervous about answering it.

Much to my delight, some of the members of my church in Christchurch invaded my cabin and decided it needed renovating. A few days later they appeared on board with a beautiful set of new cabinets specially designed for my needs. They quickly ripped out my old dresser, installed the cabinets, added a new sink and a small kitchen area and suddenly I had a new cabin. Finally it felt like home.

Just as well. The temptation to bring on board all the goods I left behind on that hurried trip to Greece was more than I could bear. The crew watched in awe as I unloaded box after box. 'Is it possible to fit everything from my three bedroom home into one small cabin?' I wondered. Ruth and Cheryl quickly grabbed the extra comforters and kitchen utensils that emerged from my supplies. Hospitality wanted my large plant containers and the library welcomed all my old books. I gladly shared around the abundance from my past life. After our visit to Guatemala, possessions didn't seem so important any more.

One of the most terrifying medical experiences I have ever had, occurred during our tour of New Zealand. All doctors I suspect, suffer from nightmares concerning the possibility of facing alone a problem which is beyond their ability to handle. Suddenly one morning, this nightmare became a reality.

We were berthed in the tiny picturesque port of Picton which nestles at the head of the beautiful Marlborough Sounds on the northern tip of the South Island. On the second morning of our visit I was sitting eating breakfast in my cabin when a panic-stricken, white faced crew member appeared. 'Hurry, hurry,' she gasped incoherently, as she grabbed my hand and quickly rushed me upstairs. Then she shoved me through the large crowd standing around one of the cabin doors.

The place was in chaos. On the floor lay the ship's husky, 6 ft 2 in physical education teacher, Mike Burnard. His body jerked erratically and white foam bubbled from his mouth and nose. He gasped painfully for breath, his face grey and his lips blue. I noticed in surprise that his hair and upper body were soaking wet. Chris MacLean and our fire chief crouched over Mike's body attempting to resuscitate him. The bathroom door was closed and behind it, I could hear the sound of cascading water.

'What happened?' I asked Chris MacLean as she busily unpacked our emergency equipment. I knew Mike was an epileptic but this didn't look like a typical fit.

The nightmarish picture rapidly unfolded. The toilet in their cabin leaked and Mike decided to fix it before going to work that morning. Suddenly the pipe burst and Mike panicked. The unexpected shock triggered an epileptic seizure which left him unconscious, with his head in the toilet bowl. Luckily, his next door neighbour was concerned by the unusual noises penetrating the bulkhead and came to investigate. Immediately she raced for help.

We dragged Mike onto the bed. His big unconscious form weighed a ton and it took three of us to manhandle him off the floor. The cabin was an appalling place in which to work. We switched on the lights. None of them seemed to work and there were no electric outlets to plug in our equipment. Thank God we had just been given a new resuscitation unit that ran on oxygen not electricity. Chris grabbed Mike's muscular arm, bracing herself determinedly against his wild thrashings while I inserted an intravenous line. At one point, he almost hurled us across the room and we wished we were burly 200 lb deckies instead of 100 lb women.

We injected valium into the vein, and sighed in relief as Mike's violent gyrations settled down. Chris clamped an oxygen mask firmly over his face and we watched anxiously as his blue lips assumed a more healthy colour.

Then the plumber arrived and attempted to open the bathroom door. He struggled for a moment, fighting against the force of the water banked against it. Suddenly the door burst open and a torrent of salt water flooded across the deck and swirled around our feet. That afternoon I noticed I had salt rings four inches up my calves. This was pioneer medicine at its worst.

By strange coincidence, one of those so obviously engineered by God, I had met the local doctor, Ron Mills, the night before. He suggested I call him if I needed help, little realizing what he was letting himself in for. An emergency call from a panic-stricken nurse early in the morning was not, I am sure, exactly what he anticipated.

Fortunately, like any good country doctor, Ron was used to dealing with emergencies. He quickly moved into high gear before racing down to the ship, he phoned the local ambulance and alerted the Blenheim police. This township, thirty-five miles to the south over a rough mountainous pass, was the closest to Picton with a hospital.

The ambulance rattled onto the dock as we carried Mike down the gangway. He was securely strapped into our brand new basket stretcher – just as well. The ambulance was an ancient vehicle designed for transporting geriatric patients. It wasn't equipped with any emergency supplies. We pushed the stretcher onto the floor and climbed in beside him.

The ambulance raced away, screeching around the windy roads towards our destination. The stretcher slipped and slid as we careered toward Blenheim and we held on grimly to maintain our own balance. Mike started to revive and his arm shot out suddenly, ripping out the IV line. It was impossible to insert a new one in the crazily swaying vehicle and we leaned our combined weight against the stretcher trying fruitlessly to keep his thrashing body in place. The ambulance roared into town and gained the grateful escort of two motorbike policemen who awaited our arrival. Their sirens blared as they screamed ahead of us, cutting a path through the early morning peak hour traffic. The ambulance careened into the hospital emergency area and we gratefully delivered our patient to the competent care of the medical team on duty.

Mike's prognosis was poor. An ugly white shadow on his X-ray indicated salt water had accumulated in his lungs. He was transferred immediately to the intensive care unit. 'He will be on a respirator for at least a week,' the physician explained. 'And in hospital for another two or three weeks.' This was terrible news. Mike's wife was five months pregnant and they were due to fly back to South Africa in ten days to await the birth. We felt helpless and useless.

Fortunately God was not so restricted. On board the ship, the news travelled fast and before we returned from the hospital, the whole community gathered to pray. God's answer was almost instantaneous. As we walked back on board, Mike's wife called from the hospital excitedly communicating that he was already awake and sitting up. He was moved out of intensive care a couple of hours later and discharged from hospital the next day. Two days later I watched as he played a vigorous game of soccer. There were tears in my eyes. His recovery was miraculous.

That was almost the last epileptic seizure that Mike ever had. His South African doctor was amazed at what had happened. It is probably not the way that I would have chosen to heal someone's epilepsy, but it was certainly very effective and had many blessings besides.

Like most doctors I was always very skeptical about the different stories I heard from people who claimed to have been healed by God. So many of them lacked confirmable evidence. Many of them just seemed to be wishful thinking. Here, however, was something I could not refute. It happened before my very eyes and consequently my faith was strengthened. For the first time I really believed that God continues to heal today.

This event had other beneficial effects as well, cementing our relationship with that local doctor from Picton. He was so impressed with our response in this crisis that he later volunteered to help during another time of need. I was amazed at the steps God is willing to take to involve those he wants to participate in his work.

One of my pleasures in being in New Zealand again, was the opportunity I had to share this beautiful country with some of my friends. The vivid contrasts with my own land of Australia, had intensified that beauty for me, not lessening my love for my native land but in fact adding to it and making me appreciate the incredible variety of all of God's creation.

In New Zealand, instead of the sweeping sunburnt plains stretching far beyond the horizon that so characterized Australia, I saw lush green paddocks dotted with fat white sheep grazing contentedly in pocket handkerchief size farms. Tall majestic snow-covered mountains, replaced the lesser ranges of Australia, tinted blue by the eucalyptus forests. New Zealanders laughed at what we Australians called a mountain, after all our highest peak was only 7000 feet. However, these ranges were made almost impenetrable by sheer sandstone cliffs and made more of a barrier to settlement than New Zealand could understand. The vast salt lakes of Central Australia, which might see rain every ten to twenty years, were a strange contrast to the brilliant blue of the glacier fed lakes and rain drenched forests of the Southern New Zealand Alps.

The South Island of New Zealand in particular holds a special place in my heart, and I was determined to share it with my friends. Eventually, I coerced Ruth and Cheryl and another friend, Lois, from the ship in Bluff at the southernmost tip of the South Island. I was anxious not only to show them part of the island but also to avoid the three day sail to Nelson. After all, New Zealand lies in the heart of the wind belt known as the Roaring Forties and the seas around it are seldom calm. I didn't want to struggle with seasickness unless it was absolutely necessary.

Lois, our newest adventurous partner, was a big tall dark haired woman, recruited from the YWAM base in New Hampshire in the United States. She responded to our desperate plea for help when the *Anastasis* crew was overwhelmed by the busy schedule in Los Angeles. Lois now worked with Ruth and Cheryl organizing functions, and directing on board activities. Her boundless energy and brisk efficiency made her a welcome addition to their team.

It was hard to prise my friends free from the hectic activity associated with organizing ship events. Supposedly there was a limit of 250 people attending each function. Unfortunately, here in isolated Bluff where little occurred to disrupt the sleepy calm of the town, the enthusiastic local helpers soon forgot that.

The day we were supposed to leave on our quick three day tour, 700 young people turned up for a youth night. They arrived by the bus load from neighbouring towns and expectantly milled around the bottom of the gangway, chatting excitedly at the prospect of the unusual adventure ahead of them. We frantically worked on a scheme to entertain them.

Ruth and Cheryl combed the ship for volunteers, recruiting anyone who could sing, dance or preach. They hurriedly put together an incredible impromptu programme. They stationed volunteers throughout the ship to keep the young exuberant visitors on the tour route and circulated them in groups – from dining room to meeting hall to video presentation. Most of them never realized the headache their exuberant presence represented for us.

Finally, late in the evening, I dragged my friends away from this chaotic event. We raced up through the rolling hills of Southland toward the majestic peaks of the Southern Alps and our first destination, Lake Wanaka. The shattered crumbly rock faces of the Remarkables, a sierra-like range rising steeply behind the popular resort town, Queenstown, glowed red and pink and yellow in the setting sun.

Next day, we hurried past the photogenic scenery, admiring the dramatic snow-capped peaks of Mount Cook at the head of Lake Pukaki. We sped on toward Lake Tekapo, an incredible turquoise blue lake that was one of my favourite places. Here David Cowie's mother, Nan, lived in an amazing hotch-potch of a house. It had grown piecemeal over the years, from a tiny single roomed holiday 'batch' to a six-bedroom home surrounded by a thick cosy hedge. Nan, a small dynamic brunette, is one of the most hospitable women I know. It was not unusual for her to cram over twenty people into her abode. She greeted our little group with open arms, fussing around us with incredible luxuries like breakfast in bed, fresh cream for our coffee and delicious homegrown raspberries for dessert. Her home had always provided a spiritual refuge for me during the time I lived in Christchurch and even on this short visit, its quiet restfulness restored all our spirits.

Hurrying further north, we ran into a storm and waded through flooded roads to our destination, Nelson. This beautiful city is situated at the base of a large U-shaped bay and surrounded on three sides by high hills. It faces north toward Cook Strait, to take full advantage of the region's abundant sunshine, though as we battled the driving rain and flooded roads that slowed our progress to a snail's pace this was not very obvious.

We arrived late, and anxiously raced down to the waterfront, convinced that all the frantic activity of ship life could not possibly go on without us. We stopped nonplussed gazing out at the windswept harbour. The *Anastasis* was not in sight. Maybe we had missed it, hidden amongst the other tiny vessels crammed into the harbour. We hunted fervently around the coastline, not considering how crazy it was to think someone could hide a vessel the height of a nine storey building from view.

The *Anastasis* too was delayed because of the storm. It was still wallowing in the high seas off the coast waiting for the winds to die down. I congratulated myself on my good fortune, relieved that I was not amongst those seasick people bobbing out there, tossed remorselessly back and forth by the waves.

Late that evening we all raced down to the harbour yet again, to watch the ship sail through the narrow channel and into its berth. We were as excited as if this was our first glimpse of her, and in many ways it was. Only Cheryl had ever seen the *Anastasis* sail into port before. It was an impressive sight. We watched, in awed silence as she sailed majestically around the breakwater and through the narrow channel, her lights blazing in the pitch black night. We were so proud of this wonderful tool God gave us to carry out his work.

By the time the *Anastasis* completed its five month tour of New Zealand, I was exhausted and ready for a break. I had not seen my family and friends in Australia for three years and desperately wanted to visit them. Once again Ruth and Cheryl decided to join my adventure. Unfortunately, sometimes, even taking a vacation is not easy.

We thought we had planned well and intended to leave about twenty-four hours after the ship arrived in Auckland, our last port of call in New Zealand. We expected to be back in time to greet the new crew and students joining us before we headed to the South Pacific Islands. During the sail to Auckland, however, our plans crumbled. The port authorities informed the captain that our berth would not be available for another twenty-four hours. Disaster! It looked as though we would miss our plane and have to cancel the whole trip.

We rushed to see the captain. 'Isn't there anything we can do to get to the airport on time?' we pleaded. He listened to our plight with a furrowed brow, unable to think of a solution. He turned to Don Stephens who was standing with him, hoping for inspiration. Don soon developed an adventurous and elaborate plan and we left with broad grins, hurrying away to pack our bags. We were delighted, but suspected the deck and engine crew would not be so impressed. It meant they would all need to be up at 2 a.m. the next morning to start up the engines and sail to the entrance of Auckland harbour.

However, we underestimated the tremendous community spirit that prevailed. Everyone was anxious to make sure I had an opportunity to visit my family and entered into the plan with great enthusiasm.

The sun rose over the horizon, just as the *Anastasis* arrived at the entrance to the harbour. It tinged the calm waters with a golden light that reflected dramatically from the distant city skyline. Cheryl, Ruth and I arrived on deck bundled in our jeans and parkas and half the crew appeared to bid us farewell. We watched as our small Bayliner motorboat was lowered into the water. Don Stephens was already on board. He had volunteered to be our chauffeur and was delighted at the opportunity to be part of our adventure.

We all clambered into the boat and sped across the slowly awakening harbour pulling our jackets tightly round us against the bite of the early morning air. The sunlight changed from gold to red and the city shone like a rose coloured jewel in front of us. We sped across the glass-like waters, past several large cargo vessels waiting, like the *Anastasis*, for an empty berth, and headed towards the dock adjacent to the customs building. The sun peeped over the buildings as we arrived. We stood in a pool of early morning sunshine warming our bodies while our ship's agent explained to the customs officer this rather unorthodox event. Another friend waited to drive us to the airport and we hurried through the peak hour traffic to our destination. We were just in time to board the plane and arrived in Sydney three hours later, a happy but rather bedraggled trio.

By the time we returned to New Zealand, the ship was ready to sail for its trip to the South Pacific Islands. Our holds were full of relief supplies to be used for cyclone relief in Fiji and Tonga. Our hospital shelves bulged with new provisions. On our foredeck several bright red fire engines were firmly tied down. They were a gift from the New Zealand Fire Department to their Fijian contemporaries.

We left New Zealand in the midst of one of the most exuberant farewells I have ever witnessed. There were hundreds of new recruits on board and an enormous crowd gathered on the dock to bid us bon voyage. Colourful streamers shot out from the side of the ship and cascaded down onto the onlookers' heads. Excited shouts and piercing screams echoed down the narrow wharf as our enthusiastic new recruits waved goodbye to family and friends. Those of us who were more seasoned travellers were less excited. A bank of thick black clouds hung over the horizon, and the ship was already heaving in the gathering swells. Outside the harbour a huge storm waited to pounce.

Once again, we sailed straight into gale force winds that sent the waves crashing against the sides and thundering over the bow. Soon everything was soaked and some of our new crew members were already regretting being on board. They lay stretched out on the floor in the aft lounge white and miserable.

On the foredeck, the vicious winds and rain lashed mercilessly at the fire engines. Water leaked insidiously through the joints and one of the engines developed an electrical short. The horn blared in raucous protest. One crew member, lying miserably in her cabin just aft of that deck could hear the noise distinctly. Her seasick befuddled brain conjured up a small boat in deadly distress ahead of us. She imagined it was signalling furiously but futilely to let us know we were on a collision course. After one particularly violent crash the ship shuddered painfully and the horn suddenly stopped. She was convinced we had hit the vessel and killed its occupants.

Fortunately, my seasick adventures were never embroidered by such a vivid imagination. All I ever imagined was that my seasick agonies would never end.

Chapter 7

SOUTH SEAS ADVENTURE

The islanders showed us unusual kindness.

Acts 28:2

Barefoot, skirt hitched precariously above my knees, medical kit clutched firmly in my free hand, I waded ashore through the mud to the tiny island of Viwa. It is one of the myriad of small islands that stretch like strings of pearls through the coral reef infested waters around the two large islands of Fiji. We had just arrived in a small motorized canoe for our first medical outreach.

Laughing, brown skinned children with black frizzy hair grabbed excitedly for our cardboard boxes full of medical supplies as we unloaded. They led us along a path that wended its way through lush tropical plantations of papayas, banana palms and mangoes. The fruit hung tantalizingly out of reach over our heads. We crested the hill and caught our first glimpse of the village nestling in the sheltering arms of a tiny cove. Corrugated iron roofs clung to walls woven from palms or to wooden huts built on stilts to allow access for the cool sea breezes. Smiling villagers waved as we passed.

ingly insignificant venture was an important milestone for me and for the whole of the medical ministry. My anticipation had been growing ever since
the *Anastasis* sailed into Suva several days before.
Choirs of native people had lined the dock to greet us,
their faces warmed by the last rays of the evening
light. White blouses contrasted vividly with dark
skins and brilliant red sashes. Their rich, melodious
voices drifted toward us through the humid air as the
Anastasis pulled into the wharf.

On board the ship we busily cleared the chairs from
the forward lounge, our largest meeting room and
waited for the church leaders to arrive. We sat cross-
legged on the floor in our white officers' uniforms
while they presented Don Stephens with a whale's
tooth hung on a necklace of tiny cowrie shells. I tried
not to squirm as my back began to ache and the rough
carpet cut uncomfortably into my bare legs. This was
an ancient traditional welcome ceremony and the
whale's tooth a symbol of friendship. I was proud to
be a part of such a moving and significant ceremony.

Later in the evening we were joined by more
church and government officials who came on board
for our arrival reception. The men appeared in their
rendition of Western business attire – white shirts and
ties with a suit jacket and matching sulu, which
resembled a wrap-round skirt, instead of trousers.
Their broad brown feet were comfortably clad in
thongs or sandals. The women wore long brightly
coloured floral dresses and cardigans. It was the
beginning of winter and the weather felt cool to them.
For us it was deliciously warm after the chill of New
Zealand.

The medical team greeted our arrival in Fiji with

mixed feelings. This was to be our testing ground. Many of the crew were still skeptical about the viability of a medical ministry such as we envisaged and did not hesitate to feed our fears and anxieties. Here in the islands, there were several small medical boats operating but no other Christian ministry possessed a hospital on a ship the size of the *Anastasis*. There were no prototypes to work with, nothing concrete on which to model our ideas and future plans. Some of the crew even struggled with the very idea of a Christian medical ministry. 'If God is only interested in saving souls, why are we concerned about curing illnesses and feeding hungry people?' they asked.

Their questions fed my insecurities. I knew God was compassionate and cared for people with physical needs, but I really had little scriptural understanding of my responsibility for people who lacked the basic essentials of living. 'Is this really your idea, Lord?' I wondered. 'Is helping people who are hungry or deformed relevant to the gospel message?' At this point I had no real answers – I needed some concrete foundations on which to work.

Now as we waded ashore on this tiny island thirty miles from Suva, God seemed to be providing the reassurance I needed. We were a small team. There was only Chris MacLean, another nurse and myself. Our chief engineer accompanied us to inspect the island's damaged water supply. Tomorrow we would return with Doug Mar for a second visit. Our objective was to examine every man, woman and child on the island. We could treat acute conditions and refer chronic complaints to the mainland for follow up. The district nurse who had arranged our visit was with us to facilitate the process. To me this outreach was like a mustard seed beginning. From this small seed we prayed, would spring a growing fruitful ministry.

We entered the village and our guides ushered us into the largest of the wooden buildings. It was empty apart from the mats of tightly woven palm fronds that covered the floor. The village elders seated themselves in the centre around a large wooden bowl that looked like a concave dish on stilts. We sat cross-legged in a circle around them and watched as the district nurse handed the headman a small brown packet: the ground-up root of a local plant. He poured the powdery contents into the bowl and added water, then stirred it. His brown sinewy fingers sloshed back and forth through the liquid that now looked like dirty dishwater.

In growing anxiety I watched as some of this extremely unappealing concoction was ladled into a half coconut shell. With much ceremony the headman clapped twice and handed me the shell. 'You must drink it down at one gulp,' whispered the nurse. 'This is their symbol of acceptance and welcome.' As the leader of the team, it was my dubious privilege to start the ceremony. I stared at the muddy looking cup in front of me. Visions of local waterborne diseases flashed through my mind. Hepatitis I knew was rampant in the islands – giardia, amoeba – who knew what lurked in the murky depths of that shell? I pushed my imaginings to the back of my mind and accepted the offering. I clapped twice, raised the shell to my mouth and swallowed.

The 'kava kava' slithered across my unaccustomed palate anaesthetizing my tongue and churning my stomach. 'It tastes like dishwater too,' I thought, as I schooled my face to an expression of appreciation. The cup passed on to the next team member and I relaxed, thinking the ordeal was over. But no! The shell passed around the circle and was soon back in my own hands. This time around it didn't taste so bad, and by the third and final time the strangeness had worn off. I felt welcomed in a very special way as I gulped down my last drink. These lovely people had accepted us into their homes, their lives and their culture. It was the first of many such cross cultural events that have greatly enriched my life.

The history of Viwa fascinated me. It was on this island 150 years ago that the Bible was first translated into Fijian. With surprise and wonder we explored the sight of the first printing press. From here, the first native missionaries carried the message of Christianity throughout the islands of the South Pacific. In their flimsy dugout canoes, they braved the fury of storms and cyclones that could toss their insubstantial craft across islands and batter them onto coral reefs. They confronted headhunters and warring tribes and penetrated the jungles of Papua New Guinea. Their efforts helped transform the Polynesian people into the gentle peace-loving islanders we met this day.

I could not believe it was coincidental that our medical ministry began on a place so significant to the story of Christianity in the South Pacific Islands. Just as the gospel grew and multiplied from this spot, so could our work.

The few days that we spent on this beautiful island encouraged all of us. We were inspired again with a desire to see the medical ministry expanded and our on-board facilities completed. Our cardboard boxes, crammed with their ill-assorted array of medications, provided treatment for skin infections and earaches but could do nothing for long term complaints. High blood pressure and diabetes were common, a consequence of high calorie and salty diets as well as genetic predisposition.

No malnutrition here. Many of the inhabitants weighed over 300 lb. They looked askance at our skinny frames and plied us with food, confiding that they would be very happy if we left the islands twice the size we arrived. Long term public health care and education were needed to change these attitudes. It started us thinking about developing community health teams that could address such concerns.

More than anything, our time on Viwa was a time of learning for me. As in Guatemala, I watched people who lived very happily without the conveniences of modern technology that we think so essential for life. There were no washing machines or even any electricity to run them, except a couple of hours a day, and there was no running water or modern plumbing. Yet the people were very content in their lives and had no desire to change.

One young man I talked to confided, 'I have plenty of food, good friends and a place to sleep. What more can I ask of life?' Friendship and community were far more important than material possessions. This sentiment was echoed later in the words of one Fijian who became part of the crew. 'You know we are so lucky on board the *Anastasis*,' he said. 'We have nice cabins to live in, hot running water for showers, electricity and good plumbing. Most importantly of all, we have good friends.'

The words of both these young men cut deep into

my heart. For the first time in my life, I started to question my Western values that place so much emphasis on material possessions. With my new-found Polynesian friends, I was more of a student than a teacher, learning from their culture the importance of being content with what I have and the value of friendship and community over possessions.

As well as this, our short visit to Viwa gave us some insights into the effectiveness of a broader approach to the gospel. The people of Viwa interpreted our efforts at medical treatment as an expression of God's love and compassion. It helped open a doorway for spiritual sharing. Several people, including the headman, were visibly impacted by the sense of God's presence in our midst. They were challenged by our commitment and hailed our visit as a time of spiritual awakening in their lives. It created in them a desire to see their island become, once again, the missionary sending base it had been 150 years ago.

Evangelism alone is not enough, I began to realize. God calls us to minister to the whole of a person's life and all of their needs, spiritual, emotional and physical, just as Christ did. He didn't just preach. He healed the sick and fed the hungry and encouraged his disciples to go and do likewise.

We returned to the ship with renewed faith in our ability to accomplish the task that still lay ahead. We looked around our medical facilities. They were undoubtedly a long way from completion. The job still seemed never-ending but the radiant smiles of the people of Viwa and the lessons they taught us, were like a beacon of hope to guide us.

Our visit to Fiji also marked a major milestone in the development of the dental ministry. All aspects of our work are intimately related and God was not letting us develop one area without the other.

Thanks to our New Zealand friend, the on-board unit was up and running and our two portable units awaited testing. Of course, as medical personnel, none of us were conversant with dentistry, but we were undaunted by our lack of knowledge. We were beginning to realize that God always seemed to conjure up the right people to help us at precisely the time we needed them. We were learning to trust him to provide.

Our three young dentists from Los Angeles came to help. They were as anxious as we were to see those dental units up and running and planned to join us for a time of ministry on the island of Vanuatu. They flew into Nandi International Airport in Fiji, their luggage bulging with dental supplies and last minute equipment purchases. We loaded their mountain of boxes into a small plane for the short hop to Savu Savu on an adjacent island. The plane skimmed across the sparkling blue ocean glistening with its network of coral reefs. The skeletons of rotting ships, picked clean by scavengers and the ravening sea, dotted the area, reminding us that this ocean is not always as benign as it now looked.

Slowly we descended toward the lush green vegetation that crowded along the coastline. I peered around anxiously as the pilot nosed towards the tangle of trees. He seemed to know what he was doing, but where was the airport, I wondered? We were almost touching the treetops before a small clearing opened in front of us and the plane taxied gently onto a tiny dirt runway surrounded by jungle. We loaded our supplies into a battered old truck and headed for the ship, eager to equip our young dentists for their outreach.

Then we heard the disastrous news. The government of Vanuatu was about to hold elections and was concerned about the impact of the *Anastasis* on the political scene. The trip to Vanuatu was cancelled.

We scurried around trying to find an alternative. Could we go to some of the small outlying Fijian islands? No! There were no boats to hire. How frustrating. Could we use our lifeboats? We used them to transport crew and visitors to and from the shore. No! They were too slow. There was no way to get our dental team to the people we wanted to help.

Fortunately our dentists were very flexible. They appeared undeterred by our sudden change of plans. As the *Anastasis* sailed to its next port, they set up one of the portable units in the ship's entryway and provided treatment for the crew, many of whom had not seen a dentist for years. They staggered back and forth with the ship's motion, peering into mouths and drilling teeth. When the motion threatened their equilibrium they hung over the side for a while watching the antics of the dolphins and flying fish that always seemed to accompany us when we sailed.

Much to our delight, Jim Mellert, who had an extra week's holiday after the others flew back to Los Angeles, did manage to travel out to one of those outlying islands. He couldn't take the dental unit with him, but with only basic supplies and equipment managed to examine and extract rotting teeth. It was an inauspicious beginning, but I felt that once again we had planted a mustard seed. We prayed it too would grow into a mighty spreading ministry.

The islands provided many challenging and

adventurous incidents for all on board the *Anastasis*. Most of our crew had never sailed in such treacherous waters before. Those skeletal old hulks I spied from the air, often marked the passageway through the reef. The peaceful lagoon that appeared to be such an inviting haven, could, in time of storm, become a hellish nightmare of whipping winds and churning waves. Many a ship had perished in an attempt to escape, their hulls pierced through by the grinding coral tentacles that now securely bound them to the reef. In Apia, Western Samoa, the *Anastasis* almost became one of them.

As in most of the island ports, the small wharf at Apia was only large enough for two or three ships to berth. We planned to stay for three weeks, and so after the first few days were asked to go out to anchor. We expected to moor the ship between two large buoys secured alongside the reef which protruded out from the island and curved around in front of the wharf. Two small tugs arrived to assist us. We stood on the deck and watched nonchalantly as they fussed around like large snub-nosed dolphins, nosing us out of the dock.

As we emerged from the sheltering edge of the island, the wind suddenly seemed to increase in volume. It roared across the water and slammed into the side of the *Anastasis*, pushing us towards the treacherous embrace of the hungrily awaiting reef. Suddenly this was no longer a simple routine manoeuvre.

The tugs' powerful engines roared as they strained fore and aft in a desperate attempt to keep us on course. They screamed in protest, battling the violent wind that tugged us relentlessly away from them and towards the reef. The ropes securing the *Anastasis* to the tugs stretched taut and one snapped as the tension increased. It snaked out with a deadly backlash that sent one of the deck crew flying, then entwined itself around the windlass, wrenched its steel bolts from the deck and carried it overboard.

I hurried down to the clinic to attend the injured crew member. She was lucky. There were painful contusions along her left side but no serious injury. I looked out of the porthole down into the murky depths of the water. The reef's razor-sharp teeth loomed ominously close. They were almost directly beneath us. On the bridge, the captain and crew fought desperately to ease the ship's bow out from behind that lethal barrier. On the deck the horrified crew watched our slow progress in silence, praying quietly for God's protection. The bow slowly edged round inch by painful inch, and finally pointed out through the reef's narrow channel toward the open sea. 'Full ahead,' the captain ordered, and suddenly we were under way, fleeing the reef's vicious tentacles.

The tugs, caught unawares by our sudden movement, protested loudly as our actions began dragging them forward with us. One vessel quickly shed its lines, but the other couldn't disengage. It dipped lower and lower, leaning at thirty then forty then fifty degrees toward the water as the *Anastasis* steamed out to sea. A cloud of black smoke belched toward us as the tug fought frantically to prevent its own demise. Suddenly our boatswain grabbed an axe and with a mighty swing severed the offending rope. Free of its tether, the tug bobbed back and forth like a cork as it righted itself. The *Anastasis* sailed hurriedly out to sea. That night we held a time of prayer and thanksgiving acknowledging God's important role in our preservation.

Half the ship's crew, about 150 people, were stranded ashore that night. Some of them had just gone for a gentle half hour stroll while the ship moved. Others had been at the beach or working with churches. None were prepared for an all night outing. They squeezed in with our onshore teams, bedding down in overcrowded tents or out under the stars. Ironically, we had all the food. The shore team had sent their cooks on board to prepare the evening meal. For them it was a lean and hungry night. On board, the throes of seasickness kept most of us out of the dining room. We had plenty of food but no appetite, they had plenty of appetite but no food.

Fortunately, I also have many fond memories of these wonderful islands to balance this nightmarish episode. The South Pacific islanders are fun loving people. As we sailed from Fiji, to Tonga, to New Caledonia, Western and American Samoa, they feasted and feted us royally. Succulent young pigs cooked underground over hot coals, fresh seafood plucked from the abundance of the surrounding waters and lush tropical fruit greeted our arrival on many occasions.

The islanders also loved to participate in our own community events and taught us much about the joy of celebrating. In Tonga, known as 'The Friendly Islands', for example, the native people helped prepare a wonderful feast for Heidi Stephens, Don and Deyon's daughter. A thirteenth birthday was always a special time of celebration for the crew children. Linda Cowie, the school's principal, had adapted the

Jewish Bar Mitzvah ceremony to mark the time when young people took on adult responsibilities and this was Heidi's time. Months before she began memorizing scripture and evaluating her commitment to God, her parents and the community. Here in Tonga, she would publicly affirm her faith, and honour her family. She lit candles on a seven pronged Menorah candlestick at each stage of this very moving ceremony to commemorate her affirmation.

Heidi's Bar Mitzvah was held outdoors on the aft deck where the gentle tropical breezes kept us cool and dissipated the clinging unpleasant humidity. Our Tongan friends festooned the ship with palm branches and hung garlands of brightly coloured flowers around the railings. Heidi and Deyon were adorned with fragrant leis that contrasted brightly with their summer frocks and fair hair.

After the ceremony, the Tongans also provided us with entertainment. They dressed in native costume – the men with dancing fronds of banana palms over their colourful lava-lavas. Their bare chests glistened with coconut oil beneath garlands of palm fronds and cowrie shells. The women wore brown wrap-round dresses made from decorated bark tapa cloth. Somehow they managed to secure them through the vigorous dances just by tucking in the ends. Red Hibiscus flowers decorated their shiny black hair. They sung and danced in their bare feet, sometimes swaying gracefully to the music, at others sitting cross-legged on the deck tapping like thunder on their drums. Some of the crew joined in as they caught the rhythm. We laughed at their stiff attempts to imitate the islanders' elegant grace – it was good to throw off our responsibilities.

In spite of these wonderful adventures, I experienced little joy or satisfaction as the ship toured the South Pacific Islands. I was exhausted after the busy schedule in New Zealand and felt unable to engender the enthusiasm I knew this time of ministry should inspire. I struggled with guilt at my lack of enjoyment and kept pushing myself to participate in more and more activities. I was convinced that with continued hard work and perseverance I would eventually break through the barriers sapping my energy and robbing my joy.

To make matters worse, I tended to spiritualize my condition, convinced that if I had more faith or greater spiritual maturity, I would not be feeling so worn out. 'If you have raced with men on foot and they have worn you out, how can you compete with horses?' (Jer 12:5) I admonished myself, compounding my guilt with self-condemnation and a sense of failure at my inability to perform in the way that I thought was expected of me. I felt distanced from God, my friends and my colleagues yet could not verbalize my fears and insecurities. I was afraid of failing to live up to my own impossible standards and experienced a growing sense of inadequacy.

I think there are times like this, for all of us when God seems harsh and far off. Not only does it appear that he allows most of the world to suffer in poverty and disease but he lays before us a thankless and unending task that reaps no reward and continually reminds us of our own inadequacies. We dare not share our fears and frustrations for fear of being found unworthy or unspiritual. It was only when the ship returned to New Zealand and I was able to take a prolonged break away from my arduous job that I began to see my problems in their true perspective. For the first two weeks of my vacation, I slept a sleep of utter exhaustion, finding I needed fourteen to sixteen hours a day to refresh my body with the rest I had denied it for so long. I got up for breakfast, staggered around the house like a zombie for a few hours, then napped all afternoon. By 10 p.m. I was ready to hit the sack again.

As I considered my burnt out condition I meditated on Elijah's sojourn in the desert as related in 1 Kings 19:1-10. He was a burnt out person if ever I saw one. The mighty miracles he performed in standing against Jezebel and the false prophets of Baal obviously drained him completely. He fled into the desert feeling alone, miserable and deserted by God. He wanted to die and give up the task God had given him. Fortunately God didn't heed his complaining. God fed him, gave him rest and refreshment, then gently admonished him. God reminded him that he had many other workers to help perform his tasks. Elijah would never be alone or unsupported in accomplishing God's work.

I felt I was receiving the same treatment. Like Elijah, and like every other one of God's creatures, I do not have unlimited energy or endurance. Like everyone else I have limits as to how far I can push myself and continue to function adequately. In my job there was no one to set those limits and I found it very difficult to say 'No!' to anyone demanding my time and energy. On top of that was the strong sense of commitment I felt to the development of this ministry on the *Anastasis*. I desperately wanted to do all I could to help people around me and the needs seemed unending. But what use would I be if I became ill or incapacitated because of my exhaustion, or if I took on my own shoulders the burdens God had given someone else to carry? I obviously needed a clear view of what God had and hadn't asked me to do. My only escape from the precipice on which I stood was a hard and honest re-evaluation of my life and priorities.

As I spent time studying the gospels I was reassured to see that even Jesus took time to draw aside from the crowds and the busyness of his task on earth to spend quiet hours in prayer and meditation with God. Christ recognized the limitations of his human body and knew when to say 'I have done enough'. He also had incredible confidence in the mission God called him to perform and so could confidently say 'no' to all that lay outside this framework.

Learning to say no to some of the constant requests and demands placed on me is probably one of the most valuable lessons I learned through that long time of rest in New Zealand. I also realized how desperately I needed to give more priority to prayer and Bible study in my life. I started to see that if I took that time in the middle of the day – which I usually thought of as 'work time' – that didn't matter, particularly when I was regularly working twelve to fourteen hours a day.

As I re-evaluated my life, I began to suspect I was in mission as a lifelong occupation, not just the two to three years I originally planned. I saw that it was important to pace myself for the long haul and not for the short term. The short bursts of furious activity I was capable of would not hold me through the years. I did not want to leave my part of God's task undone.

I think I will continue to learn these lessons

throughout my life. I constantly try to re-evaluate my progress and re-establish my priorities. The temptation to overwork and run myself into the ground remains, but I have learned to relax and take time off to enjoy the fun things I love to do without feeling guilty about the needs I leave unmet. I am learning what most quickly brings me refreshment in my body and my spirit, and endeavour to include activities in my schedule that will provide for these needs.

Chapter 8

HAWAII, LAND OF SHATTERED DREAMS

'For my thoughts are not your thoughts, neither are your ways
my ways,' declares the Lord. 'As the heavens are higher than
the earth, so are my ways higher than your ways, and my
thoughts than your thoughts.'

Is 55:8,9

I flew to Hawaii to rejoin the ship renewed in body
and spirit. As the plane descended towards Kailua
Kona on the Big Island, I spied the *Anastasis* slicing
through the white-crested waves thousands of feet
below. I was excited to be back, and eagerly watched
the tiny white toy-like speck beneath me until the
bulk of the aircraft hid it from view.

A tinge of resentment coloured my excitement.
During my absence, most of the medical personnel on
board, including my good friends Doug and Kathryn
Mar had left the ship. Thousands of Khymer refugees
were flooding across the Cambodian border and
Youth With A Mission had been asked to staff the
hospital in one of the refugee camps. Nurses, doctors
and lab technicians from the *Anastasis*, fourteen people in all, responded to this urgent cry for help.

'Why can't I go too?' I complained. 'I always wanted
to work in Thailand. Why do I have to stay behind?'

It was true. Even back in 1980, while I waited to hear from the *Anastasis*, I started planning a trip to Thailand and investigated the opportunities for medical missions in that country. I only cancelled my trip when I was accepted on the *Anastasis*. Now, once again, the opportunity to work in Thailand beckoned, and only the anticipation of continuing to develop our growing medical facilities made it possible to say no.

Then disaster struck and my struggles began anew. Shortly after our arrival in Hawaii the *Anastasis* was stopped by the US Coastguard. Originally they had agreed that the *Anastasis* could sail into American waters, just as she was, registered as a cargo vessel and without a sprinkler system. Now they changed their minds and decided the *Anastasis* could not sail again until a sprinkler system was installed.

It is not easy to retro-fit a fire system into the equivalent of a nine-storey building. Every overhead was removed to gain access for the miles of pipe to be insinuated between the already crazy network of plumbing and electrical conduits above. New metal bulkheads and fire escapes were installed. It was a mammoth task that required the recruitment of hundreds of additional volunteers. Amazingly, helpers began to arrive – first just a trickle, then a mighty river. Plumbers, welders, pipe fitters, carpenters and general purpose handymen and women responded from around the world to our pleas. Sometimes as many as seventy extra short term volunteers swelled the ranks of the long term crew.

These months in Hawaii were some of the most difficult I spent on the *Anastasis*. The hospital plans were once more on the back burner and the enthusiasm with which I had rejoined the crew was shattered in a thousand pieces.

My thoughts were constantly in turmoil as I tried to work out what I was doing stuck in Hawaii while people were dying of malnutrition and malaria on the other side of the Pacific. Regular telegrams from Thailand asking me to join the team, fuelled my confusion. Letters from friends at home questioning my staying with the ship added to my instability. Yet each time I prayed I had a strong sense that I was not to go to Thailand. 'Trust in the Lord and do good; dwell in the land and enjoy safe pasture,' Ps 37:3 leapt out at me and seemed to assure me I was in the right place. 'The Lord is not slow in keeping his promise, as some understand slowness' 2 Pet 3:9 encouraged me to believe that God had not given up on the ministry.

Sometimes this was the only assurance I had. As I wandered around the ship through the dust and dirt, I repeated the words over and over to myself. 'The Lord is not slow in keeping his promise,' I reminded myself as I looked at the deserted hospital. 'He will bring this ministry into being,' I reaffirmed as I tried to write enthusiastic letters to my questioning supporters back in Australia and New Zealand. 'This is where I am supposed to be,' I admonished myself as I thought wistfully of my friends in Thailand.

Our living situation did not help my mental state either. To satisfy coastguard requirements, the families had to live ashore. They moved from campground to campground around the island. Some resided in crowded tents and slept on the ground, others had the 'luxury' of a small cabin. All of them were cramped and uncomfortable. Yet to those of us remaining on the ship their quarters seemed like a pleasant paradise compared to the discomforts we endured.

We lived in the middle of a huge construction site. Billowing clouds of thick, acrid smoke embraced me every time I braved the passageways. Its pungent black tentacles permeated every nook and cranny, depositing a layer of fine black soot in its wake. Welders, looking like ungainly knights of old in their protective helmets and visors, patrolled the corridors. Their bodies, totally encased in black leather suits, were eerily silhouetted against the blinding white light emitted by their sizzling acetylene cutting torches.

Opposite my cabin, piles of debris obstructed the narrow passageway. This was the site of a major valve station. I needed the agility of a mountain goat to clamber over growing piles of rubble and long sections of new pipe to my home. Eventually a ladder was set up for me to scale the mess. Dust settled everywhere, and I gave up the unequal struggle to keep my clothes and books clean. Eventually, as the teams moved relentlessly onward, my haven too was invaded and ripped apart. I became a refugee in my own home, fleeing from cabin to cabin ahead of the construction teams which seemed to set their beady eyes on my new abode the moment I became comfortable.

The hospital looked like a war zone on a bad day. The bulkheads we had so painstakingly scraped and painted back in Greece were blackened and chipped beyond recognition, their paint blistered by the intense heat of the welding torches. Dismantled overheads littered the decks exposing the ship's stark metal skeleton and its disorderly array of pipes above. We unearthed old yellowed paper hats and Italian graffiti behind one panel. The newspaper was dated 1952. No one had moved these panels since the ship was constructed.

Small deadly drops of molten metal flew in all directions as the welders set to work. Burn marks honeycombed the old blankets we protectively spread over our precious equipment. Hardy patients pushed aside heavy tarpaulins and waded through the debris to attend clinic. I gained a new area of expertise – the removal of small metal chips and the resultant rust rings from eyes. These were a constant hazard, particularly when workers forgot to wear their goggles.

Even at night there was little relief from the dirt and debris. Car transports sailed into Pier 39 opposite us, like ghostly skyscrapers, and disgorged their fleets of gleaming new cars all night. The sound of revving engines and screeching wheels echoed in the tunnel between the ships. Drivers manoeuvred like racing car experts in their efforts to unload as quickly as possible.

On other horrifying occasions, cement ships berthed opposite us, sometimes for six weeks at a time. The fine grey powder that filled their holds was unloaded with what looked like a giant vacuum cleaner. An ear-splitting noise reverberated through the *Anastasis* all day and all night, robbing our sleep and shattering our nerves. It could be heard three miles away. In my cabin on the starboard side, I shouted to make myself heard and slept with earplugs to reduce the thunder to a gentle roar. In the hospital on the port side, the bulk of the ship muffled the sound but the noise still penetrated our bones and threatened to rob us of our sanity.

None of this helped create a positive impression of Hawaii for me. For years I was one of her worst tourist advertisements. The mere mention of the name Honolulu conjured up images of Pier 39 with its nightmare of cement and cars. Flying dust and clouds of grey powder obscured my view of palm trees gently swaying in the balmy tropical breezes.

Fortunately, local Christians took pity on us. They invited us into their homes and churches. They fed us and gave us places to relax and regain our equilibrium. They prayed with us and encouraged our endeavours. For Ruth and I, it was Clarence and Bernice Oshita, a Japanese couple from Moanalua Gardens Missionary Church, who became our ministering angels. Their hospitality was amazing. Every Sunday for eighteen months they faithfully arrived on the dock to take us to church. Then they drove us home and fed us on bacon, lettuce and tomato sandwiches. Sometimes we flopped exhausted on their living room sofas and slept the afternoon away. We always returned to the ship relaxed and able to cope with another gruelling week.

There were also lighter moments on board to liven our existence. For most, Hawaii is the land for honeymoons – for us it seemed to be the season for weddings. Romances blossomed all over the place, and every few weeks there was a fresh celebration on board. Sometimes the aft deck was festooned with palm leaves and flowers, a nostalgic reminder of more tranquil days in the South Pacific. On other occasions the ceremony was a more traditional Western affair with the bride glowing brightly in her flowing white gown and the groom and attendants resplendent in formal dress uniforms.

One wedding was even held at sea. The docks were crowded with cruise ships, and there was no room for us to remain at the wharf. Early on Saturday morning the *Anastasis* was towed out to anchor for the weekend. Across the water from us, the majestic volcanic cone of Diamond Head glistened in the early morning sun. Its stark rugged beauty contrasted strongly with the sparkle of Waikiki beach and the artificial glitter of its towering buildings. Suddenly a cry went up from the bridge 'Whales on the port bow' and we all raced outside to view these enormous barnacle clad creatures as they gracefully slid by.

What an idyllic setting for a wedding, I thought. Unfortunately, as the day progressed, the lazy Pacific swell increased and the ship began to roll uncomfortably. By the time the wedding started we were all fighting hard against the rising nausea. Our assistant director, Nick Savoca, was officiating. He bustled around beforehand making sure all the guests and wedding party were well fortified with seasick pills. Alas, in his thoughtfulness Nick forgot his own weakness. As the ceremony progressed, his face took on a decidedly green hue under his shock of black hair. Sweat broke out on his brow, and he struggled valiantly to complete his duties. Nick bent over the communion cup then hurriedly straightened his 6 ft 5 in frame as a wave of nausea threatened to engulf him. He quickly completed the ceremony and headed for his cabin. It may not have been the most spectacular wedding on board but it was certainly one of the most memorable.

At first, it was hard for me to concentrate on these lighter moments in the midst of my unfulfilled expectations. Then slowly I began to see the glimmer of light at the end of the tunnel. Even in the midst of the sprinkler system onslaught, the medical ministry continued to develop. My struggles were not in vain and maybe it was true – 'The Lord is not slow in keeping his promise'.

As the welders and pipe fitters moved through the hospital, their cutting torches slashed into the metal bulkheads creating jagged gaping holes. These marked the emergence of new doorways and windows. The padded cell, used in the ship's ocean liner days to confine psychiatric patients or felons, was ripped apart. Its yellow upholstery and tiny stuffy aspect was guaranteed to make any sane person mad anyway. This became the foundation for our new pharmacy with narrow shelves and clear plastic doors – just right for displaying the myriad of sample medications.

We gutted one of the bathrooms to develop our new nurses' station, replacing the cumbersome old tub with gleaming white wall to wall cabinets. One of those jagged holes became a large picture window, opening it up to the waiting patients.

Then we began work on the sterilizer room. It housed what looked like a decompression chamber – an ancient sterilizer big enough for blankets and mattresses. We never even attempted to use it, afraid that we could cause an explosion. The welders cut it in sections and removed it from the ship piecemeal, then cut a hole in the bulkhead to gain access for our new machine that stood waiting in the corridor.

It was also during this time that an extremely important prayer meeting was held that dissipated my despondency and gave me new hope to focus on.

Don and Deyon were concerned about the development of the medical department and called together the captain, chief engineer, medical team and other key leaders to pray about the future. We met in our partially completed conference room, surrounded by piles of dirt and rubble. God's presence was strongly in our midst reassuring and encouraging us. 'One day this will be the heart of your ministry,' we sensed he was saying to us. 'One day it will provide the lifeblood to sustain all your efforts.' It was as though God lifted the curtain a little and gave us a glimpse of the future. For the first time we were all in agreement as to the importance of the hospital and its ministry.

This glimpse of the future left me with a terrible sense of my own inadequacy and of our need for a variety of new resources. There was no way our present tiny team could prepare for what lay ahead. Accomplishing our vision would take far more than the meagre resources we now possessed.

Cynthia Carr, a dental therapist from Ireland, heralded the first of our new personnel. She is a born administrator and was key to the development of the whole dental ministry. Cynthia bounced on board with a mischievous sparkle in her blue eyes and an infectious smile on her freckled face. She radiated good humour like a restorative tonic and soon teased all of us out of the doldrums. Nobody could be despondent when Cynthia was around. With her ready organizational skills and a liberal dose of the Irish blarney, she talked the plumbers and carpenters into completing the dental room. Then she recruited short term volunteers to work on the crew's dental needs.

Unfortunately, Cynthia's addition to our team

made me more, not less, aware of my own ignorance and inadequacies. We needed doctors and nurses skilled in plastic surgery and ophthalmology who could both advise and participate with us in the ministry. We needed a bank of workers interested in short term involvement who could supplement our long term staff with their skills and expertise. Most of all we needed finances and equipment to see the hospital adequately prepared for surgery. When I started considering the extent of our needs, I was almost overwhelmed. There was so much we lacked and much time and effort was still required to see our dreams come true.

With this in mind, I began to plan a trip to Europe in order to increase my knowledge of our ministry, recruit volunteers and broaden our support base. Ruth Crow, my faithful partner in many adventures would accompany me as guide, translator and companion. She had lived in Switzerland, France and Belgium, spoke fluent French and a smattering of German, and knew Europe intimately. How grateful I was for her expertise and help.

This trip was a real faith venture as neither the ship, nor Ruth and I, had enough finances to provide for our airfares and other expenses. We pooled our meagre resources and the ship provided some support but there was still a big gap. Panic! I could never identify with those great people of faith who trusted God to provide without even seeming to turn a hair. I read stories of people who waited at the airport until God miraculously provided a plane ticket. It only made me feel more inadequate. Did they worry for weeks beforehand as to whether God would provide? I certainly did.

My weight dropped down and down as I endured the suspense of 'trusting God' for his provision. When we prayed, an intense sense of peace settled over me. 'Come, all you who are thirsty come to the waters; and you who have no money come buy and eat!' Is 55:1 came to my mind. How appropriate! As long as I concentrated on God, and his faithfulness as expressed in this scripture, I believed we would have all we needed for our trip. The moment I concentrated on our need my stomach churned and my confidence dissipated.

The money slowly dribbled in. We took up an offering on board and anonymous gifts began appearing in the mail. We inched closer and closer to our goal. The church we attended contributed too and prayed for us. The day for purchasing our tickets dawned and we nervously counted our resources. Amazingly, there was just enough to buy one-way tickets from Hawaii to Belgium, our landing place in Europe. That was all we needed at this stage. We had speaking engagements in LA, Florida and South Africa that would provide additional capital on the way, but nothing was certain. There was no turning back, if God did not provide we would be stranded on the other side of the world.

God's initial mode of provision seemed to set the pattern for the whole of the next few months. There was always just enough money to provide for our needs, yet we rarely had much left over. We bought additional plane tickets to Scandinavia and England, rented a car to travel around Europe always using our last pennies for the purchase. Each time we started to worry an unexpected offering replenished our meagre resources bringing with it a sense of

God's encouragement and reassurance.

Amazingly, we returned to Hawaii with almost the same amount of money we set out with. For both Ruth and I, it was a wonderful learning experience regarding God's provision. Firstly, I suspect God only provides like this when we are stretched beyond the limits of our natural resources. God is not limited by our projected budgets and obvious cash flow. If we had not been willing to risk stepping out beyond our own meagre resources we would never have seen how incredibly faithful God can be in such a situation.

Secondly, I also think that such a miraculous flow of finances only occurs when we require it for the work of God's kingdom not for the fulfilment of our own wants and desires. In 2 Cor 9:8 God promises us 'all that you need, you will abound in every good work.' Unfortunately, we often get so hung up on providing for ourselves first, that we cannot see what we have as provision for every good work. This trip taught me to concentrate more on God's provision for the things we are called to do and be, than on my own needs.

Amazingly, along the way, God blessed us incredibly as well. We drove through the majestic mountains of Switzerland with their postcard scenery and doll house chalets. We gasped in awe at the fairy tale lands of Scandinavia just before Christmas. And we ended that trip by spending Christmas in Switzerland with Ruth's family. It was my first ever white Christmas, an opportunity to learn to ski and to enjoy luxuries that most of us only ever dream of.

This was a very fruitful trip practically as well as spiritually. Within a few weeks of our return, a

Belgian dentist arrived in Hawaii to help Cynthia in her newly completed facility. And even today, medical personnel who were first encountered during that crazy escapade still write and ask about opportunities on board.

Most unexpected of all, it was during this adventure that we first met Gary Parker, a young maxillofacial surgeon from California. Gary worked in Northern Wales. He drove for three hours through torrential rain to a meeting at the YWAM base in the British Midlands. He unwound his long lanky frame from his tiny Morris Mini and tried to unobtrusively enter the meeting. His 6 ft 3 in frame, black hair and bushy beard made him conspicuous in any setting however. We were soon deep in conversation. We were impressed by his gentle compassionate spirit and deep concern for the less fortunate of the world. His expressive brown eyes sparkled with enthusiasm as we shared our hopes for the future of the medical ministry on the *Anastasis*. When we left, Gary was hooked and ready to join our first surgical team.

Gary's name stayed in my mind for many months. It sprang instantly to the forefront when we were preparing for our first surgical venture. He has since played a key role in the development of the Mercy Ships ministry and has now lived on board the *Anastasis* for several years. I doubt we would ever have met him if we had failed to risk our security and comfort by embarking on that crazy trip.

Avidly embracing this new project and turning my back on the opportunities I so longed for in Thailand, I almost missed the Lord's next step for me and a blessing he bestowed just before our trip to Europe. A telegram arrived asking me to spend a month in

Thailand, while Doug and Kathryn had a holiday.

I could hardly believe God was reopening a door I thought firmly closed and it took me a while to recognize that this time his answer was a resounding 'yes!' This time, however, I was not going to stay. The experience would better equip me to share the needs of our desperate brothers and sisters around the world. God's timing was perfect yet again. Now I could share compellingly concerning God's heart for the poor and his purposes for the *Anastasis* as a tool to answer those needs.

Chapter 9

BLUE PLASTIC AND BAMBOO HUTS

For God will deliver the needy who cry out, the afflicted who
have no one to help. He will take pity on the weak and the
needy and save the needy from death. He will rescue them
from oppression and violence, for precious is their blood in his
sight.

Ps 72 : 12–14

I think I will always look at Thailand through rose
tinted glasses. I feasted my eyes on the ornate golden
spires of Buddhist temples that speckled the landscape. They glinted in the brilliant sunlight as I made
my way from Bangkok to Aranypratet on the
Thai/Cambodian border. Enormous water buffalo
with dirty grey hides and long ferocious horns plod-
ded placidly along the roadside beside their weary
owners. Waterlogged rice paddies stretched unbroken on either side. They were dotted with the bent
over figures of women in broad brimmed conical
hats, planting and weeding. Occasionally the bus
passed a fisherman casting his long bamboo pole into
the paddy's murky waters. Only the discordant jan-
gle of Thai music, high pitched and monotonous to
my untuned ear cast a shadow over my exciting first
impressions. It reverberated through my head

throughout my five hour drive.

My romantic vision did not protect me, however, from the overwhelming impact of the desolate refugee camps. Rows of tiny bamboo huts crammed thousands of people into a couple of square miles of dusty, brown space. Their palm frond roofs were patched with bright blue plastic that flapped disconsolately in the breeze, adding a splash of colour to the depressing landscape. The huts squatted close to the ground away from the deadly bombs that sometimes whistled overhead. Khaki clad soldiers walked past with sub-machine guns slung nonchalantly over their shoulders. Their presence was a stark reminder of the violence that could erupt at any minute putting an untimely end to our ministrations of mercy.

The hospital was no better. Shards of light cast through the bamboo slats, dappling the stark wooden palettes we used as patient beds. In the dim light above, hung ragged lines of patient charts and bottles of IV fluids. Emaciated wide eyed infants swung listlessly back and forth in tiny hammocks. Their piteous cries drifted weakly across the milling crowds toward us. The hot, humid air was filled with the smell of sweat and urine. There was no electricity, no running water and no sanitation. Outside, an array of sandbags provided the semblance of a bomb shelter, another reminder that we were working in a war zone. But with many of the patients using it as a latrine, who would dare hide there except in a state of greatest extremis?

Nothing had prepared me for the impact of the constant panorama of heart-rending sights parading before my eyes. Television specials made everything so unreal. At home, the agony, the degradation and the pain of displaced peoples didn't seem real. Divorced from the dirt, flies, heat and constant painful sounds of suffering, the video camera placed an invisible barrier between me and the tragedy I watched. Now suddenly, it was all real. 'These are flesh and blood people,' I realized with shock. 'Just like my friends and my family. Their emotions are just like mine. They laugh as I do, cry as I do, and grieve for their children and their families just as I would mine.'

New arrivals from Cambodia dragged their emaciated infants to the hospital. Their disease ridden bodies were listless and unresponsive from severe malnutrition and debilitating disease. Distended, pot-bellied abdomens bore silent witness to the parasitic infections running rampant in their tiny bodies. Puffy hands and red hair bespoke calorie and protein deficiencies. The spectre of tuberculosis hung constantly over us with many new cases arriving each day. Painfully we turned many away. Treatment could only be given to those who had become part of the camp's stable population. A minimum of six months was required. Disrupted treatment would only add to the problem. How do you say 'no' when by so doing you may as well be signing a death sentence? I agonized.

One ten-year-old girl was carried in by her mother. She only weighed 25 lb (11 kg). Her puffy, stick-like legs and weakened constitution made it impossible for her to walk. She stared at me with big brown unhappy eyes through her dull, unkempt black hair. Her once beautiful face reflected more pain and suffering than any child should have to endure. She was severely malnourished, riddled with tuberculosis, parasites and who knew what else. My eyes filled with tears as I ran my hands over her listless body. It was doubtful that our limited facilities could save her life.

Another child, Bu, a two-year-old infant was admitted to the hospital, following a bout of diarrhoea. Her parents only brought her to us reluctantly as a last resort. Several months before her older sister had died from a similar illness, and the family in their ignorance, blamed the nasal feeding tubes and Western medicine for her demise. Now Bu was malnourished and dehydrated. She screamed as she caught sight of our white unfamiliar faces. 'White devils' some of the Cambodians called us. It was not easy to break through the prejudices.

We spent hours working with Bu and her mother who had already given up hope of her daughter's survival. Pain and grief were etched on her face as she held the precious infant in her arms, vainly trying to tempt Bu with small sips of fluid and her favourite foods. We sat on the wooden palette beside her, surrounded by small plastic bags full of life-giving electrolyte solutions. We held the mother's hand, encouraging her to feed her irritable, dying child. More than anything we encouraged her to love and care again and helped her regain the hope she needed to promote her daughter's survival.

Then one day, almost three weeks after her admission, Bu reached out of her own accord for the boiled egg in her dish. For the first time for weeks, she was hungry and greedily devoured her meal. We grinned and clapped our hands. Tears ran down our faces as we watched the mother's eyes light up with the promise of new life. Years later I heard from one of the long term workers in the camp that Bu grew up to become a bouncing normal teenager, with no obvious outward scars left by the tragedy that almost deprived her of life.

The refugee camps also challenged my dependence on modern technology. I will never forget the day Eileen, our maternal child care nurse, rushed from the clinic exclaiming 'We just delivered premature twins. They weigh only 3 lb each.' I looked at her in dismay. What hope did we have of keeping these tiny infants alive without a baby incubator or other modern aids?

Fortunately Eileen had a good dose of Irish practicality. She was far more innovative than I and quickly sprang into action. She scavenged one large and two small cardboard boxes from the pharmacy and rummaged through the garbage for half a dozen empty IV bottles. Then she grabbed an old worn blanket from one of the wards, and unearthed a roll of aluminium foil from our supplies.

Eileen sat the largest box on the floor and carefully filled the IV bottles with boiling water. She lay them in the bottom of the box and placed the two small boxes in on top. Eileen gently wrapped the babies in a layer of foil and snuggled them into the blanket as a final layer of warmth. Amazing! We had our innovative incubator, and the babies thrived.

It was hard to see God in the midst of the suffering and pain around us. It was even more difficult to understand why he allowed innocent children like these to bear the pain of our sinful world. Yet in our midst he surely was. Patients dying of malaria and TB saw visions of Jesus that transformed their last moments into a haven of peace and joy. Workers and patients alike, were challenged by the claims of Christ on their lives. The love of God seemed to shine in our midst, and though we were not allowed to share our faith openly, lives were touched and changed by the care we showed. Through the disruption and turmoil of their lives, many refugees came to a living faith in God and a hope of eternal life through Jesus Christ, his Son.

At the same time I knew God was disrupting my life through these experiences and continuing to chip away at the complacency and indifference in which I had cloaked myself. Building on the foundations begun in Guatemala God was transforming my attitude to the poor and to people in need.

As I listened to the agonizing stories many of the refugees told about their flight from the nightmare Pol Pot perpetrated, I was appalled by the pain and suffering they had endured. Until now, I had always assumed that people were poor because they were lazy or uninterested and that we had no responsibility to change their plight. In the refugee camps, that was obviously not true and I started to wonder about my whole attitude to those less fortunate than myself. For the first time in my life, I was forced to step beyond concern for my own comforts and security to reach out to a far greater need that I could no longer ignore.

One particularly challenging book I read was Ron Sider's *Rich Christians in an Age of Hunger* [1]. As he says: 'According to scripture it is just as much a part of God's essence to defend the weak, the stranger and the oppressed as to create the universe. Because of who he is, Yahweh lifts up the mistreated. The foundation of Christian concern for the hungry and oppressed is that God cares for them.'

As I read Ron's book, I discovered to my amazement, that the scriptures often spoke about the poor
and the needy and encouraged God's people to be
concerned for them. From Genesis to Revelation we
are reminded again and again to remember those less
fortunate than ourselves. Isaiah, Jeremiah, and
Ezekiel, in fact all the Old Testament prophets, cry
out in condemnation against a people who are
greedy, and neglectful of the alien, the widow and the
poor.

'Speak up for those who cannot speak for themselves, for the rights of all who are destitute. Speak up
and judge fairly; defend the rights of the poor and
needy,' proclaims Prov 31:8–9, piercing my heart with
the cry from those who are helpless.

I was shocked as I read the judgement that often
comes because of transgressions in this area. Prov
21:13: 'If a man shuts his ears to the cry of the poor, he
too will cry out and not be answered.' Many other
scriptures like it address this issue in a succinct and
inarguable fashion. Amazing to me, even the sin of
Sodom and Gomorrah, in my mind associated with
sexual transgression, related to their neglect of the
poor. 'Now this was the sin of your sister Sodom: She
and her daughters were arrogant, overfed and unconcerned; they did not help the poor and needy. They
were haughty and did detestable things before me.
Therefore I did away with them as you have seen' Ez
16:49.

The New Testament too, continually reminded me
of this responsibility. Christian faith goes far beyond
the preaching of spiritual salvation. It is a message for
the whole person, a promise of succour in physical,

emotional and spiritual realms. Faith is nothing without action, as James so aptly portrays.

> What good is it my brothers, if a man claims to have faith but has no deeds? Can such faith save him? Suppose a brother or sister is without clothes and daily food. If one of you says to him, 'Go, I wish you well; keep warm and well fed,' but does nothing about his physical needs, what good is it? In the same way, faith by itself, if it is not accompanied by action, is dead.
> Jm 2:14–17

My findings in scripture were underlined by other reading. According to the World Health Organization, half the world's population lacks the basic necessities of life. They have no clean water, no decent house in which to live and no access to even basic health care. They live in constant threat of death and disease. Most devastating of all I read in David Barret's *Christian Encyclopaedia*, 200 million of these desperate people are Christians, my brothers and sisters in Christ. Many more, even in our Western societies, live in a cocoon of loneliness and isolation, beset by emotional deprivation and despair.

I felt angry and frustrated as I contemplated the results of my studies. Need is all around us, I admitted, yet I was oblivious to the desperation of my fellow human beings. I was as unaware of the lonely person across the street as I was of the starving child on the other side of the world. And worst of all I had no sense of responsibility to these people.

My encounters in Thailand taught me that ministry to the poor and needy is not an alternative to the gospel of Jesus Christ for those who are afraid to witness, neither is it a political alternative, for those who seek social change. It is an integral part of the Good

News. We cannot preach the message of eternal salvation without feeding the hungry and healing the sick. This is the mandate that the Lord proclaims to all of us as Christians.

In those four short weeks of service, my life was changed forever. No longer could I see my own personal fulfilment as the most important occurrence in this world. Having touched the pain and suffering that is such an overwhelming aspect of life I was challenged to see my own skills and faith as an extension of God's love and concern for all people. I saw the hope of redemption, not only as an answer for myself but for the whole of humankind in its sin and degradation.

The scripture that most radically impressed me and which has become a kind of symbol of responsibility for me is 1 Jn 3:16–18. It proclaims its message in the very heart of this book on Christian love.

> 'This is how we know what love is: Jesus Christ laid down his life for us. And we ought to lay down our lives for our brothers. If anyone has material possessions and sees his brother in need but has no pity on him, how can the love of God be in him? Dear children, let us not love with words or tongue but with actions and in truth.'

This verse disrupted the values on which my Christianity was based. I started to realize that God does not bless us with prosperity, education and health to squander on our own self-centred ambitions. The challenge of Christianity is to look beyond our own comforts to the hurt and dying world outside. It was imperative for me to free my spirit from the burdens and encumbrances of the material world and be willing to embrace the concepts that are truly important in God's eyes. Christ was willing to give up the wonder and glory of heaven to enter our pain racked world and more incredibly to die a painful and agonizing death to free all humanity from the burden of sin and death. How could I be willing to do less?

As a young Christian I learned to quote Jn 3:16: 'For God so loved the world that he gave his one and only Son, that whoever believes in him shall not perish but have eternal life.' I embraced its message as an encapsulated form of the whole gospel. It strengthened my faith in the love of God and focused my eyes on the wonder of eternity spent in communion with Christ. Now it occurred to me that this verse really only represented half the gospel message. I believe 1 Jn 3:16–18 represents the other half. To me, these verses complement each other. They are incomplete separately but together are more powerful than any other thoughts we could express. Physical salvation is no good without the message of eternal salvation, but neither is the hope of eternal glory adequate when our bodies are suffering and dying for lack of food and water.

Working with the refugees in Thailand was never easy. Many had suffered atrocities that destroyed their material security leaving them angry and acquisitive. They stole constantly. Nothing we left lying around, from bamboo benches to pens and paper, was safe. Even patient medications were pocketed for sale on the black market. On one occasion some young boys even dug holes under the bamboo walls to get into the pharmacy. Sometimes the refugees resented our presence and even more so, our freedom to come and go as we wanted.

To us, the refugees were selfish and lacked concern for their fellow sufferers. We resented their ingratitude and sometimes wondered why we bothered to care for such difficult people. Yet we could see our love slowly piercing the protective shells in which they encased themselves.

It is never easy to work with oppressed and displaced people. Their suffering and pain, if untouched by the love of God forms almost impenetrable barriers. We constantly struggle against the sinful nature of man and the greed and selfishness it imposes. Only the love of God can penetrate such shields. And in the process our own faith and ability to love and care grows and moves us toward a deeper relationship with the God whom we serve.

Chapter 10

PHYSICIANS ON TRIAL

See! The winter is past; the rains are over and gone. Flowers appear on the earth; the season of singing has come.

Song of Songs 2:11–12

'This is the nicest 522 foot refrigerator I have ever lived in', grumbled one short term volunteer as he donned a fourth jersey to keep himself warm. After eighteen months of hard work on the sprinkler system, we had sailed from the balmy tropical weather of Hawaii to Victoria, British Columbia, for the coldest winter they had experienced in forty years. The work was not completed but had reached the stage where we needed access to dry dock facilities to continue.

'You will love Victoria,' our Canadian friends assured us. 'It is one of the most beautiful parts of the country. The weather is never really cold and it hardly ever snows,' they explained, aware that some of us were a little nervous of the fact that we were sailing north in October.

How wrong could they be? For several weeks on two separate occasions, the *Anastasis* and its crew shivered in below freezing temperatures under a thick, powdery white blanket. Snow encased our decks and covered our equipment, smothering us with its icy embrace. Long pointed icicles sparkled from the overheads, and the watery sunlight glinted dimly through the ice-encrusted portholes into our frozen cabins. Even a glass of water left by the bedside at night, froze. Our power supply was limited and the heating system was only turned on for an hour in the morning and another in the evening. The warmth dissipated quickly through the ship's metal sides and into the chilly water outside.

Fashion went by the board as we bundled ourselves into anything warm. We raided the second-hand boutique for extra layers of jerseys, socks and thermal wear unconcerned by the ragged cuffs or mismatched colours. My sheepskin coat and boots became permanent fixtures and I knitted furiously to increase my supply of woollen garments. We clasped hot-water bottles to our roly-poly, overdressed frames and waddled around the ship like penguins, our bodies shivering and our bones aching with the penetrating cold. Around us, the concrete bulk of the graving-dock stood grey and bleak against the pale winter sky. This was to be our home for another year until the renovation was completed and the *Anastasis* passed inspection.

Work on the hospital inched forward and we turned our attention to the growing mountain of supplies in one of the ship's cargo holds. It was not a pleasant task, particularly for this time of the year. The inky blackness of the hold crowded in around us sucking out the heat from our icy bodies.

Doug Mar, our faithful inventor, was back on board. He had returned with his wife Kathryn, from Thailand, just before the *Anastasis* left Hawaii. Sadly for me, this would be their last visit. They returned to Thailand early in 1986 for an extended stay. The vision they had so enthusiastically shared would come to fruition without their encouraging support.

However, we thanked God for Doug's inventive creativity during this difficult time in Victoria. He hung searchlights from the hold supports and we huddled round our sorting tables in a small puddle of light. He excitedly unearthed a motley collection of old heat lamps from one of our treasure trove of boxes and secured them beside the lights. He lugged old mattresses down from the hospital and suspended them around the tables. He filled in the gaps with old smelly tarpaulins that emitted a greasy oily aroma as they warmed under the lights. We didn't care. They blocked the whistling wind and gave us some relief from the penetrating cold. Our fingers cracked and bled in the dry uncompromising air. They were stiff and unwieldy inside their gloves and frustrated our efforts to sort small packets of sutures, dressings and icy instruments.

Four months of bitter wintry weather engulfed us before the glory of spring-time burst forth with its profusion of new life. New leaves, as lovely as any flower, glimmering translucencies in a thousand shades of green and gold, red and copper, blue and silver. Shrubs and trees overwhelmed us with their heady fragrance from blossoms of pink and red and yellow. And bulbs, thousands of them, all beautiful, pushed their heads up through the chilly earth. Splashes of daffodils, sunny and golden, waved in the wind, washing away the last traces of winter's reserve. Proud exotic tulips in every colour of the rainbow followed behind, their bold colours dancing in interlacing clusters around the gardens.

Suddenly Victoria was all it was meant to be, dispelling forever that gloomy frozen picture forming in my mind. Hanging baskets filled with trailing ivy, blue lobelia and brilliant splashes of red, pink and purple petunias and geraniums were hung from lamp-posts as the weather warmed. The old Empress Hotel, festooned with a rich coat of ivy, basked proudly in the summer sunlight. Flocks of tourists in baggy shorts and tee-shirts invaded from many lands inquisitively exploring the quaint Victorian buildings and their vibrant floral displays.

As the weather improved and the spring of 1986 burst into bloom around us, we too seemed to burst into new life. Once again the *Anastasis* was undergoing a rebirth, and this time the medical ministry was being birthed with it. 'See! The winter is past; the rains are over and gone. Flowers appear on the earth; the season of singing has come,' we were reminded from Song of Solomon 2:11-12 and so it seemed to be.

The devastating Mexican earthquake of September 17th 1985, now provided a focus for future ministry. It smashed through Mexico City early one morning, toppling buildings, destroying hospitals and burying hundreds of people in its deadly embrace.

Chris MacLean, recently returned from Thailand, was there within a couple of days to evaluate the possibility of ship-related teams becoming involved. She established a base in Lazaro Cardenas on the west coast of Mexico, close to the epicentre of the earthquake. Over the next year, while the ship continued its slow progress toward completion, she co-ordinated construction workers and outreach teams which arrived to help repair the tumbled mess. And in the medical department we began to plan our first medical and dental outreaches.

Friends started to visit Victoria and our hearts stirred as that intangible dream that had drawn us through the graveyard experiences of the last six years took on form and substance.

Will and Nadine Davies were the first to arrive. They bustled on board with their usual enthusiasm and exuberance, undaunted by the blistered overheads still lining the hospital corridors. They inspected our newly installed autoclave and exclaimed in excitement at the developing pharmacy and operating area. Soon Bill appeared in striped overalls and a red bandanna. A baseball cap covered his woolly curls and a pair of dusty goggles were pushed up over his forehead. A metal grinder hung limply from his right hand and a broad grin spread across his face. With glee, he attacked the metal posts and obstructions which blocked progress in our new clinic area on the level below the operating rooms.

Then Dr Bob Dyer hit the scene. A well-established ophthalmic surgeon from San Diego, Bob was restless and dissatisfied with his work. Initially he ignored the Mercy Ships literature appearing on his desk. After all, what could a surgeon in his mid-fifties with greying hair do with an outfit calling itself Youth With A Mission? Eventually, however, our persistence paid off. The thought of working on a ship, strange though this one sounded, fired Bob's imagination. On top of that, he had a desire to use his medical skills for people without hope of adequate treatment. He decided to investigate.

Bob flew into Victoria immaculately dressed in an expensive new sports suit and a crisp white shirt.

How he survived his first demoralizing view of the eye examining room, I will never know. He surveyed the mess through metal framed spectacles that glinted in the dim light and ran his fingers along the grimy surfaces. The metal deck was rusted and dirty. Its integrity was severely jeopardized by several jagged holes which availed a wonderful view of the sewing room below. The dirty white bulkheads were streaked with years of accumulated grease and grime. One wall proudly sported a large irregular gap through which the printing press, the room's previous occupant, had been removed. The other was piled high with dirty bags of cement and pink and yellow rolls of fluffy insulation. An old rickety fan was propped precariously in one porthole. Nothing could have been more desolate or depressing. 'Eye room?', I am sure he wondered. 'Eye of faith room more likely!'

Amazingly, Dr Bob, as he soon became known, was not deterred by this initial unsavoury impression. He pushed the bags of cement around the room, his brow furrowed with concentration. In his fertile imagination, they represented examining chairs and instrument tables. Dirty rags identified patients or staff members. Bob's eyes glowed with the zeal of a born visionary as he vividly described his ideas to us. He loved architectural drawing and design and covered sheets of yellow foolscap paper with graphic sketches and detailed plans.

Cynthia and her dental team also raced into action. Theirs would be the first health team leaving the ship for Mexico. With great enthusiasm they assembled the portable units and fired up their generators. They oiled the drills and meticulously counted burr heads and anaesthetic cartridges. We purchased an old grey van and loaded it high. Portable dental units, generators, dental supplies as well as food and personal items were crammed aboard until it looked as though the van would burst at the seams. It had a long haul ahead. It was almost 4000 miles to Lazaro Cardenas. Our dentist Dr Richard Ruhe volunteered to drive, along with Kit Wahlander, one of our nurses from Sweden. Several short term volunteers would join them in Mexico.

I flew down to Lazaro Cardenas to meet the van and its travel-weary team. My heart was almost bursting with excitement. Our adventures in the South Pacific Islands were nothing compared to this. Not only would our dental units finally be in action helping people in need, but during my visit I would also meet with local hospital officials to plan a surgical outreach. In some ways it seemed absurd. We still had no hospital on board, no surgeons and little equipment or supplies, but somehow we believed it was possible. God had planted a seed in my heart and nurtured it through the prayers of Doug and Kathryn, Don and Deyon and the others who had unwaveringly believed in this ministry. I had a growing conviction that this was God's timing for the start of our ministry and nothing could shake that assurance.

Lazaro Cardenas itself, is not the most beautiful Mexican city, not by any stretch of the imagination. It is a recent invention built around a man-made port and industrial complex. Wide, dusty modern streets, liberally seeded with huge muddy potholes, embraced the town with their busy network. Ragged children skipped into the roads at every intersection, pushing their wares through the car windows or trying to clean our windshields. Smartly dressed businessmen sidestepped the street vendors who crowded the sidewalks with their overflowing baskets of highly coloured wares. Wizened old ladies squatted beside tiny charcoal fires cooking corn or tortillas to tempt the passersby. Away from the main streets stretched rows of concrete houses pressed close to the ground behind protective walls and iron bars.

Outside the town, squalid villages clung precariously to the brown hillsides. Tiny hovels of tar paper and rusty iron roofs, interspersed the more permanent wood and mud structures. Occasionally a concrete block building stood stark and grey beside its fellows. Mexico wore her cheapest perfume in this quarter and the smell of her body was rank and shameless where the poor and homeless were crowded together. Garbage littered the streets along the open sewer. It was damp and stinking – a favourite haunt for pigs, goats and dogs intermingled with children playing.

Not far away was Ixtapa. Here opulent new highrise hotels encroached greedily on the white sandy beach. Parasails dappled the bright blue sky with flashes of gaudy colour. Bikini-clad tourists lazed contentedly beside sparkling swimming pools negligently shooing away the beggar children who plied their wares along the beach. This was a different world and the contrast was unbelievable. We strode uncomfortably through the artificial glitter trying to reconcile it with the stark reality of the villages hidden just minutes away.

Our dental team established itself in a dilapidated

old hotel further along the coast at Playa Azul. Here, white paint peeled untidily from the slowly decaying building and dark patches of mould spotted the walls. The team's rooms looked out onto an empty swimming pool beyond which the dirty white sands stretched. The beach was lined with small outdoor cafes that sheltered under palm-thatched open canopies and beckoned temptingly to the few daring tourists fleeing the glitter of Ixtapa.

From this humble base, the dental team ventured into the surrounding countryside driving their dusty grey van up the hill each day to Respuesta Sociale which in English means 'The Social Answer'. Here, the village elders lent us part of the community centre, and our team set up their two portable dental units. Patients presented themselves hesitantly at the door unsure of their welcome. Children peered through the bamboo slats at the unusual sight, exclaiming at the shrill high-pitched whir of the drills and deafened by the roar of the portable generator. They grinned in delight as their teeth were repaired. No one had ever come to help them like this before.

This first outreach was not easy. We were inexperienced and unsure and our team consisted of a bare minimum of people. Our supplies were limited and our help only scratched the surface of need. However, it was a start, and we rejoiced and praised God for what we were able to accomplish.

From there, I descended on the hospital in Lazaro Cardenas, eager to plan a surgical outreach. I was shocked at the mess. Its debris-strewn interior could have doubled for the *Anastasis* at the height of the sprinkler system renovations, but on a much larger scale. The earthquake had caused extensive damage and now it was being rebuilt by a Swiss relief agency.

We walked across the hospital's brown tiled floors, our footsteps echoing eerily along the almost deserted corridors. Concrete pillars rose like the bleached bones of a gigantic skeleton around us and the hot humid air wafted unpleasantly through its open sides. This was all that remained of the badly cracked and damaged walls. We glimpsed the wooden doors propped against palm trees in the courtyard waiting to be rehung. We peered into the X-ray room. It was covered with rubble and plaster, a tarpaulin hastily draped over the expensive equipment. Its oversized electrical cables hung dangerously over the table. The operating area was temporarily closed, its insides gutted and awaiting reconstruction. Rooms were stacked high with supplies and equipment donated by the Rotary Club.

We met with the hospital director who seemed puzzled by our interest and cautious about our offer. Could there be enough cleft lips and palates in the area to keep us busy for six weeks? Hesitantly he agreed. The arrival of our surgical team would provide a wonderful way to commemorate the reopening of the hospital.

I returned to the ship eager to venture out into this first surgical outreach. Busily we once again raided our treasure trove in the hold, piling up sutures and dressings and surgical instruments. We contacted our meagre list of recruits praying for the right people to join our team.

My letter to Gary Parker, that eager young maxillofacial surgeon in Wales, crossed in the mail with his letter asking me about upcoming opportunities. He agreed to meet me at the airport in Los Angeles and fly down for the full six weeks of operating. Will Davies signed on for a week of burns surgery. Pam Mitchell, a nurse well experienced in burns and reconstructive surgery responded from New Zealand. She would come to help organize and set up the outreach. Praise God for someone who knew how to treat cleft lips and palates. Frieda Dorman, a surgical nurse from England was already at our port office in Los Angeles, trying desperately to add to our meagre stack of supplies. She would head up the operating crew. Our team was taking shape.

Other volunteers also responded to our cry for help. Slowly a team developed. The numbers would be barely adequate for the work we anticipated doing. Some could just come for a few weeks, others would participate in the whole outreach.

Some were called in unusual ways. One young man signed up after he heard a ship advertisement on television. Strangely, as far as we know, nothing like that was ever screened. Yet that non-existent advertisement challenged him to join our team and later he and his family spent many years working in missions. God obviously had his hand on the preparation of this small team and each person appeared to be hand-picked. This was very definitely his team, not ours.

I boarded the plane in Victoria with two enormous suitcases crammed with last minute supplies and instruments. Pam, Frieda and a small team of helpers were already in Lazaro Cardenas anxiously awaiting our arrival. Over the last couple of weeks, a steady stream of faxes, letters and phone calls had helped us fill in the details necessary for this momentous first surgical outreach. Now, ready or not we were about to begin.

Gary joined me in Los Angeles and settled in beside me as the plane took off for the last leg of our trip to Mexico. It was time to get acquainted. 'When do the other surgeons arrive?' he asked as the plane trundled down the runway. 'Other surgeons?' I looked at him blankly. 'You're our only one' I explained nervously. Somehow in the midst of our numerous letters and phone calls that fact had remained unmentioned. He looked at me in horror, his face draining of colour under the black beard. 'I'm the only surgeon . . . but didn't I tell you I have very little experience with cleft lips and palates. I was hoping to learn from other surgeons more experienced with this particular operation.' Somehow that fact too had not emerged.

Over the next couple of days Gary pored nervously over his books, muttering under his breath as he painstakingly performed numerous phantom operations. His hands flashed back and forth, hovering over an imaginary patient as he tried to visualize the intricate steps involved. He cut out pictures to hang on the wall and drew diagrams to assist him. He fingered his instruments anxiously and sorted out what he needed. None of us could help. Like me, most had never even seen a cleft lip. 'Lord, are we crazy?' I wondered. 'Is this really your idea?'

Slowly we began to relax and Gary's confidence grew as the steps for the procedure became familiar. After all, the principles were the same as the other, often more complex reconstructive operations he performed. There was nothing to worry about, was there?

Then came our screening day. Thirty-five hopeful

patients awaited our arrival at the hospital. They lined the corridor like participants in a macabre sideshow. Most of them looked down at the floor or held their hands over their faces in shame. Infants in arms, small children, young adults and old folk all with one thing in common – a gaping hole split their faces from upper lip to the base of the nose. In some the palate was missing as well and we looked straight into their nasal cavities. They spoke with guttural, unintelligible voices. In others the gap was on both sides and the flattened nostrils flared out widely and grotesquely above it. The teeth protruded forward, deformed and ugly.

Gary and I were overwhelmed and gulped in dismay as we beckoned the first patient forward. Nothing had prepared us for such an array of maimed and tragic people. Tears sprang to our eyes as we peered closely into their distorted faces. Sad hopeless eyes stared back at us. These people were the rejects of their society, cast off and neglected. They were used to disdain and ostracism and had little hope we could change them.

Gary hung his pictures in the operating room and meticulously set to work. I was his nervous assistant. Dressed in my baggy blue scrub suit and paper hat that often hung askew over my right ear, I peered over his shoulder. I pulled gently on the delicately placed retractors and cut the incredibly fine but strong sutures. I anxiously watched the intricate rearranging of tissues, fully absorbed in the beauty of the reconstruction taking place under Gary's careful fingers.

The surgical nurses, looking very efficient in their floral scrub sets, expertly spread out the surgical packs and handed Gary instruments and sponges. The circulating staff scurried round unearthing last-minute supplies and the recovery crew waited expectantly for their first patient. A translator stood ready to help us communicate with the patient and the Mexican staff. We looked like a well-oiled and efficient team. It was hard to believe we had never worked together before.

The Mexican nurses and doctors watched in fascination. Most of them had never seen an operation like this before either. They listened to Gary's explanation, asking questions continually. They were eager to learn. Soon they too were involved and vied with our nurses for the opportunity to scrub for the operations. Gary solved the communication problem with a mishmash of English and broken Spanish that had all of us chuckling quietly.

We soon realized that working in an environment like this offered all kinds of challenges we had never faced before. The meagre supplies and equipment we brought with us represented an overflowing abundance to the Mexican staff. They greedily grabbed our old syringes and cast-off tubing, resterilizing and reusing items until they became brittle and unusable. The anaesthetist hovered protectively round our offerings of endotracheal tubes, his eyes gleaming behind his mask at the unexpected windfall.

Out in the ward, there were more lessons to learn. Beds often had no sheets and the patients slept on the bare bloodstained mattresses. The nurses surreptitiously dried their hands on their skirts, embarrassed by our shocked expressions. At first our nurses were horrified and quickly depleted their supply of paper towels in the effort to adhere to our Western ways.

When these ran out, they turned to cloth towels but soon learned the laundry could not cope with the extra volume. Hesitantly they too began to adapt. The day our nurses first wiped their hands on their skirts was a red-letter day for the Mexican nurses. They smiled encouragingly, accepting us now in a way our foreign standards and practices had made impossible.

We learned much from their enforced frugality, too, humbled by the Mexicans' acceptance of conditions we refused to accept. The Mexican nurses taught us to economize with supplies, helping us make maximum use of all we brought. They showed us how to improvise when necessary and above all, taught us to be grateful for what we did have rather than grumbling about what we didn't.

Other challenges too kept us learning rapidly throughout this first visit to Mexico. It wasn't easy to adapt from the efficiency and task oriented nature of a Western hospital to a more relaxed relationship based situation. Every morning we arose, resolved to start our work on time, at least once. Every day, some new obstacle stopped us achieving our goal. One morning the hotel staff forgot to fix breakfast. By the time we roused them from their beds and had them bustling round the kitchen, we were already an hour late. On another occasion, there was no power at the hospital and we waited impatiently for its reconnection. Sometimes the water was turned off, or the autoclave didn't work and we had no instruments. At times the patients were late, or an emergency operation delayed us. We became angry and frustrated by the slow pace.

'Why don't you take time to talk to us?' the hospital

staff asked one day as we impatiently paced back and forth in the empty recovery room. 'You're always too busy,' they admonished us, their brown faces puckering with concern. They wanted to ask about our families, our lives and our faith. All we seemed interested in was our work and how to make our procedures more efficient.

Their complaint was justified. In our Western society getting the job done tends to be far more important than making friends and developing relationships. We love numbers and statistics and tend to judge our efforts in quantities not qualities. To the fun-loving Mexicans, as in most seemingly underprivileged cultures, relationships are more important. To the hospital staff, it didn't matter if we performed thirty-three or thirty-four operations. What mattered most was how involved we became in their lives, and how much interest we showed in them as people. We all needed to slow down and learn to listen to the people around us, just as our Mexican friends were able to do.

We learned lessons regarding our faith as well. On one occasion, Gary developed diarrhoea in the middle of an operation. He grew paler and paler as his condition slowly deteriorated and his temperature rose. Sweat poured down his brow in his determined effort to finish the operation. The staff hovered anxiously round offering him sips of water and mopping his brow. I watched him nervously, aware that if he couldn't continue, I would somehow have to complete the procedure.

Finally nausea and dizziness overcame him and Gary collapsed on the operating room floor. His face was ashen grey and his skin cold and clammy. We crowded round him in concern, laid hands on him and prayed. As we did so, Gary's headache and nausea suddenly abated. He rose with new energy and was able to rescrub and complete the operation.

For many of us, it was the first time we really depended on God for the performance of our professional skills and we were amazed at how he honoured our prayers. Gary continued to struggle with diarrhoea over the next few weeks, but he felt God had miraculously intervened when we prayed to enable him to complete his important task.

Our faith grew steadily throughout the outreach. We started each day with a time of prayer and worship that bonded us together as a team far more quickly than we thought possible. Often, as we shared our frustrations and our insecurities, God's presence hovered over us in a tangible and very special way. Without him we knew this outreach would never have been possible.

Our prayers continued throughout the day. We prayed with each patient before they were anaesthetized and then throughout the operation. Our non-medical translators often took the lead in this important contribution to our efforts. We prayed again in the recovery room, and often shared the incredible privilege of praying with the patients and their families as they rejoiced in the transformation brought about by the operations.

We learned much from our patients and their families too. Antonio for example, was one of our first patients. At three years of age, his teeth already protruded grotesquely through his gaping cleft lip. Unconcerned by our constant prodding and poking, Antonio mischievously clowned around in a sombrero and cowboy boots as we examined his lip and broken palate. After the operation he strutted around the ward swinging his nasogastric tube – his elephant's trunk – back and forth.

His mother often prayed with our translators. She looked at his new face, still puffy and swollen, and wept at the transformation. Ever since his birth, she had prayed for this. We were astounded at the tremendous faith that had sustained her through her son's ordeal and ostracism. In our intervention, she was very aware of the love of a God who cares for each individual person he created. Her testimony made us aware of the importance of this part of the gospel. God very definitely does call us to reach out with his love to people in need.

Marta, a sixteen-year-old girl with a bilateral cleft lip was one of our most memorable patients of that first outreach. Her big soulful brown eyes burned into the depths of all our souls. Hopelessness clung to her like a depressing blanket. Her sack-like brown dress and lank untidy hair showed that her hideous deformity had robbed her of all pride in her appearance.

A two-hour operation transformed Marta's life forever. Three months later when we returned for a follow-up visit, all that remained of her childhood trauma were two thin scars. Her eyes sparkled with light and her face glowed with new vitality. A radiant smile split her face from ear to ear as she walked toward us in a new stylish black and white dress. We asked how the operation had affected her life and her eyes welled with tears. She was speechless. No words could tell of the changes in her life. Because of her operation Marta no longer hid in the house. Now she had friends. Shortly she would be married.

As I watched Marta's glowing face I realized how easily we could have cancelled this outreach and left her and the other patients we treated in misery for the rest of their lives. Gary with his pictures – me completely ignorant of cleft lip and palate surgery – all of us with a motley collection of mismatched instruments and inadequate supplies. None of us were properly prepared. None of us knew all the right things to do or the right things to say. Thank God we had listened to that still small voice prompting us to believe that this was the right time and the right place to begin our surgical ministry and that each of us had a part to play in its accomplishment.

When I stopped to think about it, faith was the element that made this outreach possible. Faith was what had made it possible for all of us to pursue our dream even when it seemed impossible. It meant we could trust God to fill in the gaps in our inadequacies. Because of our faith, established through times of prayer and meditation with God, we could step beyond our comfort zones into the unknown, believing that God would accomplish all he wanted to through our lives. Now, as I looked at Marta'a face, I knew the truth of that verse from 2 Peter that had been my only support during our months in Hawaii. 'The Lord is *not* slow in keeping his promise.' This was his place, his people and his timing. All we had needed was faith and a willingness to persevere through the hardships.

Chapter 11

READY OR NOT WE OPERATE

Then will the eyes of the blind be opened and the ears of the
deaf unstopped. Then will the lame leap like a deer, and the
mute tongue shout for joy. Water will gush forth in the wilderness and streams in the desert.

Is 35:5,6

I returned to the ship in Victoria, walking on air,
enthusiastic to communicate what we had accomplished. I never imagined the impact a cleft lip operation could have on a person's life would be so
dramatic. The images of those brilliantly smiling
faces, transformed forever by a simple operation,
were indelibly etched in my mind.

The eager crew listened with bated breath as I
showed my slides and shared my stories. For them
too, it was the beginning of a dream come true. Their
efforts, and those of everyone who had worked on
board since the ship was purchased in 1978, had
made this all possible. Together we rejoiced at the
glimmer of a new era for the ministry.

More than that, the sprinkler system was now completed and the *Anastasis* was ready to sail. The long
wait was finally over. Now the ship too was ready to
embark on its first significant shipboard medical mission of mercy.

Hospital construction progressed with renewed zeal as the ship sailed down the west coast of the US. The workers swarmed over the operating area like busy bees, fitting new doors and windows, installing cabinetry and refinishing the battered and bruised bulkheads.

The welders and plumbers, their skills freshly honed on the installation of the sprinkler system, attacked the overhead panels yet again. Soon, thin copper pipes snaked along the corridors through the overhead space and into the operating room. These were our new anaesthetic lines. Huge oxygen and nitrogen cylinders were lugged into a tiny musty closet along the corridor, and hooked up. We turned on the anaesthetic machine, and watched the indicator knobs drift from empty to full. Now we were beginning to feel like a hospital.

The little room that Dr Bob Dyer had so meticulously measured and planned started to take shape as well. Fresh white paint and new white cabinets replaced the grease and grime. The welders secured solid metal plates over the gaping holes in the deck and we moved in our eye-examining equipment. In the centre stood a bright yellow examining chair. It reclined backwards with barely an inch to spare between it and the back bulkhead. A bright pink stand swung out from one wall. This provided a secure mount for the slit lamp through which the ophthalmologist examined the patient's eyes. Not great colour co-ordination, but no less functional for that.

By the time we reached San Diego and Bob reappeared on board, the eye room had undergone an amazing transformation. It was unrecognizable as the mess he had last viewed. Now it was an eye room indeed.

The construction work inched forward too slowly for my taste. 'Can we possibly be finished on time?' I wondered anxiously surveying the mess that seemed to increase every day.

Our visits to Olympia, San Francisco, Los Angeles, and San Diego, punctuated by that mad sail described in Chapter 1, all passed in a mad flurry of activity. Now we were fighting against time to have our facilities operational and our supplies ready before we reached Mexico. Equipment slowly accumulated as we sailed on. Anaesthetic machines, an operating microscope for eye surgery, patient monitors, and lab equipment were gradually marked off our long list of needs. We prayed daily for God's provision, rejoicing in each new donation as another indication of his incredible faithfulness.

The nurses ordered surgical gloves, overshoes and operating gowns. Green paper wrap littered the conference room as they frantically packed instrument trays, surgical drapes and scrub gowns ready for the big day. Dusty boxes from the hold disgorged their prized array of sutures, medications and dressings as the newly installed cupboards were stocked. Staff at the home office in San Pedro, California worked overtime in their valiant efforts to convince pharmaceutical and supply houses to donate the goods we needed. It was hard to apprise them of our needs when we had never even performed a single operation on board.

Suddenly I too had a new and challenging role. Now to my job of construction supervisor, crew physician and outreach co-ordinator I added that of public speaker and chief recruiter. It was rather daunting to speak to medical and dental groups, Rotary clubs and church meetings, endeavouring to recruit their help with volunteers or supplies or finances. I worked hard to convince them that the debris-filled facility they now visited would soon become a fully operational hospital. It wasn't always easy, and many walked away shaking their heads in despair. Sometimes I felt I wanted to join them.

In San Diego, to add to my insecurities, I caught a glimpse of what a hospital ship could really look like. On our arrival, we sailed past the newly built *Mercy*, an enormous naval vessel, freshly outfitted and gleaming with new paint and a brilliant red cross on its side. It was built for the US Navy, to handle war casualties. The *Mercy* sat in its dock awaiting its first assignment. This was a hospital ship 'par excellence' and it bristled with the latest in expensive hospital equipment.

The Admiral invited us on board, and we were soon drooling in envy. Stainless steel benches and instrument trays gleamed bright and new. The multiple operating rooms overflowed with sophisticated monitors and the very latest in anaesthetic equipment. Much of it was still shrouded in plastic wrap. The recovery area sprouted oxygen tanks and TV screens like an enormous intensive care ward. It glowed with the fresh, new antiseptic sterility one would expect of any modern hospital. Wide spacious corridors led between the wards and the recovery rooms, silent and musty. A helicopter pad dominated the aft deck. A long spiral ramp provided rapid access to the hospital two storeys below. It was all a little overwhelming.

The next day, the Admiral reciprocated our visit. He appeared at the *Anastasis* gangway, his smart white uniform dripping with gold braid and impressive medals. The *Mercy* was on its way to the Philippines for a humanitarian mission and the Admiral wanted our advice. He had never worked with the poor on a mission like this before and seemed to think that I was the expert in running hospital ships.

With great embarrassment, I led him down our dirty narrow passageways and into the hospital area still littered with battered overheads and construction equipment. He surveyed our single tiny operating room decked out in its second-hand equipment. He looked askance at the rickety old army stretchers balanced on their wooden legs that were our patient beds. I tried to explain our work and the faith that had sustained us all through the years of preparation. He admired our dedication and commitment and congratulated us on the job we were undertaking. I am sure, however, that he wondered at our audacity in calling this a 'hospital ship'. I know it made him grateful for the abundant resources he had access to.

The *Anastasis* sailed out of San Diego on our last leg of the trip to Mexico on a beautiful crystal clear morning. We watched the city recede behind us as wisps of early morning fog swirled up from the calm blue sea.

I surveyed the hospital in alarm. The electricians and carpenters were still hard at work and it was only five days until our arrival in Lazaro Cardenas, ten days until we were due to operate. The nurses waited anxiously for the construction to finish. They still needed to scrub and sterilize the whole operating area and the boxes of goods to be autoclaved looked like a small mountain. We prayed daily for the completion of our facilities and all the last minute details. At times this was all that kept us believing it really was all possible and that in just a few days we really would begin operating.

Finally, the pipes were all hooked up, and steam gushed through on its way to the autoclave. It pounded past the air pockets like some huge percussion orchestra and hungrily engulfed the first load of supplies we dragged out of the bulging store room. Clouds of hot steam billowed around us and up toward the overhead as we pushed open the thick steel door on our first experimental load. Suddenly a spray of cold water drenched us from above, flooding the corridor and dribbling down through the deck to the cabins below. The sprinkler system, triggered by the heat, had decided to go into action. At least we knew it worked! But we would rather have found out in some other way.

By the time we sailed into Lazaro Cardenas, everyone on board was involved in the last minute hospital work. Volunteers from every department and children from the ship's school appeared at all hours, sacrificing their leisure time, to help pack last minute supplies and sort the ever present boxes of sample medications. Our newly recruited short term medical staff who had boarded the ship in San Diego were also hard at work. Even Dr Gary and Dr Bob, who had come aboard just before we sailed, were soon scrubbing down walls and applying last minute coats of paint.

We pulled into port and a new wave of avid volunteers from the deck and engine departments immediately joined our willing workers. The electricians and deck crew hung over the side busily installing our two tiny air-conditioners. These perched on small shelves suspended outside the operating room and eye room portholes. The cold draught of air they emitted, slightly eased the dripping humidity and clinging tropical heat. The hospital A.C. power supply was insufficient to run the units so a special generator was installed on the foredeck. Bright orange electrical cords snaked up the side of the ship, past three decks of portholes and over the rails to connect them.

Even the chief engineer and captain appeared to give a hand. They joined the cleaning team down on their knees scrubbing away the greasy marks and accumulated grime of the sprinkler system days. Toothbrushes, scrub brushes, rags and buckets were all employed in our frantic late night exploits as we toiled energetically to accomplish our task.

Finally, less than twenty-four hours before we were due to operate, the last work crew wiped down the last piece of equipment and headed out the door. Our hospital, with its single tiny operating room and three-bed ward, was finished. Dr Bob and his operating team were poised ready to perform the first surgery ever, on board the hospital ship *Anastasis*.

I could hardly believe it. It was almost seven years since I first arrived on board the *Anastasis* back in Greece. Seven years of hard work and doubts and difficulties but seven years too of experiencing God's incredible faithfulness and love. Years of learning to trust him, realizing that when things do not work out as I expect, God has not abandoned me. 'The Lord is not slow in keeping his promise', and this was the incredible beginning of the fulfilment of all he promised us.

The crew watched in awe as the first patient, an elderly grandmother called Sophia, made her way shakily up the gangway. Her eyes were clouded with the milky white cataracts that had robbed her of her vision years before. She settled herself in one of the army stretchers lining our tiny ward, while her daughter hovered nervously by. Sophia's brown wrinkled face, anxious but hopeful, peered up at the nurses as they explained the unfamiliar procedure. She couldn't write, but pressed her thumb, covered in red ink, firmly onto the patient consent form. Then she donned her yellow paper gown and tucked her greying hair into a surgical cap. The daughter watched anxiously as the nurses led her down the corridor and into the operating area.

Inside the hospital we all waited expectantly. Anyone with the least excuse to be present crowded into the operating area. I looked around at this amazing team God had so incredibly brought together.

Dr Gary hovered around helping with last-minute preparations. He had taken a course in anaesthetics during his training and was supervising this critical part of the procedure. A local Mexican anaesthesiologist was on board to work with him. Julia Martin, a surgical nurse from South Africa, was scrubbed ready to assist Dr Bob. Her small, intent figure leaned over the instrument tray as she checked her supplies. She was well experienced in eye surgery and confidently waited for the operation to begin.

Dr Bob positioned himself behind the operating microscope and called for silence as we prayed. I held my breath as he commenced the delicate operation. The words from Isaiah 35 ran through my mind.

'Then will the eyes of the blind be opened', I murmured as Bob slowly and expertly removed the offending lens and showed us its sight-stopping opacities. I watched in awe as he inserted the new lens and closed the incision.

Once again, God was fulfilling his promises. The words of hope that had guided us for so long were being fulfilled in front of our eyes. My eyes filled with tears as we prayed again, thanking God for the wonderful miracle of bringing new sight to those who could not see.

The next morning we once more raced down to the hospital and crowded round in growing anticipation as Bob removed Sophia's eye patch. With a dramatic flourish, he waved his hand in front of Sophia's eye and she gasped in amazement. 'I can see! I can see!' she exclaimed excitedly, grabbing Bob's hand in a delighted handshake. She turned towards her daughter, fondly examining the beloved face she had not seen for seven years. Tears ran down her face. 'Gracias, gracias (Thank you, thank you)' she murmured as we bade goodbye and waved her down the gangway.

That was the first of many operations Bob and his colleagues performed on board the *Anastasis*. A steady stream of patients, some old and frail, some young and hopeful staggered up the gangway each day seeking new sight and a new life.

One family – the Teles family – had several children blind from birth. Bob operated on each in turn and we stood round afterwards praising and thanking God for his provision. The youngest child, a ragged three-year-old, sick of our prayers pulled impatiently at his father's hand. 'When can I go outside to see what the world is like?' he asked. The sea, the land, trees, houses and cars – they were all new and exciting and he gazed in awe at the incredible sights his new vision revealed.

Bob also performed strabismus surgeries. Young children walked shyly on board, gazing at us crookedly through their crossed eyes. They peered round nervously at the unfamiliar ship sights and squatted by the beds playing tentatively with the toys we provided. Soon they were joined by some of the crew children who shared their own toys with these new-found friends. Each child left the ship with a cuddly toy for their very own, something most had never owned before.

The morning after the operations, surrounded by his usual crew of onlookers, Bob again stripped away the bandages to reveal perfectly normal eyes that now focused straight ahead. Mothers clapped in delight when their bewildered children, still smarting from the pain of the procedure, gazed at them with bloodshot but straight eyes. For them we may not have restored sight, but we had given them back the chance of a normal life.

Now that the new facilities on board were christened, Gary began work once again in the local Lazaro Cardenas hospital. Each morning he and his surgical team loaded themselves and their growing mountain of equipment into our light blue VW van and zoomed through the docks and across the town to their work. Patient monitors, electrocautery machine, sutures, dressings and medications were all lugged up to the hospital each day and returned to the ship at night. It was a far cry from those meagre supplies we made do with on the previous trip. A two-way radio system was set up to facilitate our communication.

Gary and I greeted old friends from our last visit with great delight. Marta was there radiating the joy of her new life and Antonio raced up to meet us, his brown face alive with mischief. He was back for a second operation on his cleft palate. New patients too heralded our arrival.

Rafael the shoe-shine man came hesitantly to see us, encouraged by some crew members who met him in the street. At first he refused to believe anything could be done to remove the ugly cleft lip that marred his face and disgraced his life. He was in his fifties and had lived his whole life looking down at people's feet. Being a shoe-shine man meant he never needed to look them in the face. He wouldn't look straight at us either. After the operation, however, it was a different story. He arrived for his follow-up examination in a dapper new suit and smart little hat. 'Now I know that God lives and cares for me,' he told us. 'Through your help God has worked in my life.'

Dr Will Davies and his wife Nadine were back on board for a week too. For them, as much as for us, this was like a dream come true. Before we left Los Angeles, Will had packed his bright orange metal trunk with dermatomes, burns dressings and special creams, and loaded it on board. We kept our eyes open throughout the screening process for patients with burn scarring.

The day Will arrived, a young man brought his bewildered four-year-old daughter, Maria, limping in to see us. Two years before, her plastic crib had caught fire engulfing her in a sea of flames. A massive sheet of puckered scar tissue coalesced across her back in a broad ugly swathe. It glued her upper arms tightly to her sides from elbow to shoulder in a vicious embrace. Another ridge of thick scar tissue ran the length of her left leg, twisting it backwards like a club foot. For two years Maria hadn't been able to lift her hands above her head or skip and run like a normal child. She looked scared and miserable, obviously severely traumatized by the tragedy.

Maria's family lived in a remote village many miles from Lazaro Cardenas. Yet even there, they heard rumours about the *Anastasis*, the white ship that was performing surgery free of charge. They travelled for hours, first down the river by canoe, then through the dusty back roads on a donkey, and finally on a bus to Lazaro Cardenas.

Maria and her father arrived travel worn and dusty at the hospital, pleading anxiously for help. It was amazing that they appeared on this of all days, the very day that coincided with Will's short visit on board. He scurried down to examine her, running his fingers along the scars, stretching her distorted limbs and evaluating her situation. There was plenty of time to operate and follow her progress through the healing process. God was obviously at work in the timing of her visit.

On this and a subsequent trip to Mexico, Will performed two extensive operations on Maria, freeing the scar tissue that so disfigured and confined her body. Today she looks like a normal child, running and jumping and waving her hands around like all her little friends.

Cynthia and the dental team also headed out from the ship each morning across the town and up the hill back to the village of Respuesta Sociale. She was wonderfully supported by a dentist from San Diego who sailed down with the ship for the whole six weeks of the outreach.

Rolinda Lee was a tall elegant woman in her mid-thirties. Her golden curls bobbed rhythmically up and down as she worked to drill away decay and to insert amalgam fillings. Her face glowed as she attacked yet another needy mouth. 'This is what I came into dentistry for,' she said to me, her eyes shining with enthusiasm. 'I cannot imagine doing anything more satisfying with my professional skills.' The words echoed in my mind. As I surveyed the patients here and on the ship, I too knew that this was God's purpose in bringing me into medicine. I could imagine nothing more satisfying to accomplish with my life than to reach out and help those who are unable to help themselves.

Rolinda participated in several outreaches on board the *Anastasis*. Her deep, sincere faith and glowing testimony were an inspiration to many on board. Tragically, shortly after her return from her last visit, Rolinda developed cancer and died several months later. When I learned of her death, my mind returned instantly to those words. How wonderful it is for any of us to discover God's purpose for our skills before we die.

Each day as the dental team sped up the dusty road and past the ramshackle wood and tar paper houses, heads appeared at windows and doors. Our team's arrival was still greeted rather suspiciously by these people who weren't used to free dental or medical care.

Most of the inhabitants had been displaced by the building of a new dam. They fled the rising waters hoping for work in Lazaro Cardenas's growing industrial complex. They were disillusioned by the government and saw their own efforts as the only solution to their problems. It was hard to believe that people from a distant country could really care for them, and they wondered what our hidden motives could be. They cautiously allowed the team to set up their units in the local community hall, surrounded by its communist posters and propaganda.

The headman's wife, Talma, came to supervise. Her short dumpy figure bristled with suspicion and she glared threateningly at the gathering patients who crowded eagerly round the clinic doorway. She yelled angrily and officiously ordered them into line as the dental work began. She was bitter and critical as a result of a life of rejection and suffering and was concerned that our staff might try to adversely influence the people.

Talma's piercing black eyes missed nothing in the clinic. She peered over Cynthia's shoulder watching the examination of rotting painful teeth. In one corner, Dr Joe Lubcome, an oral surgeon from California, sat surrounded by an assortment of chisels and forceps. Talma watched impassively as he extracted rotting irredeemable teeth. She inspected the bleeding gaping holes thoughtfully.

At the back of the long room, one of the dental assistants was hard at work. Talma watched in fascination as she washed out gloves in chlorox bleach so that they could be reused. Beside her a small sterilizer steamed merrily away preparing instruments for the next patients. Through the wall she could hear the roar of our compressor standing outside surrounded by a horde of inquisitive, chattering children.

Talma was intrigued and astonished by this unusual group of people who claimed to come in the name of God. Marta, our little friend with the cleft lip also came from this village and Talma already knew of the wonderful transformation that had occurred in her life. She watched surreptitiously as the team ministered to her people, intrigued by the loving attitude and dedicated concern of the dentists. She sat by the patients still waiting to be examined and watched and rewatched the film *Jesus* that continually played in the waiting room. Then she began asking questions about this God who cared in more than an impersonal, disinterested way.

What most touched and changed Talma was the story of a young medical student from New Zealand who was, for a short time, part of this dental team. Ian Wallbridge, long and lanky, with light brown hair and an intense, serious face behind his gold-rimmed glasses, came to the *Anastasis* for a three month elective term. He wanted to learn more about medical missions. Ian started work with Dr Gary up at the hospital, then rotated onto the ship's surgical team, became part of our medical team and finally wound up on the dental team for a couple of weeks. He spent hours bent over Dr Joe's shoulder learning to pull teeth. He was certainly learning about every aspect of medical missions.

Ian was deeply affected by the poverty and degradation in the villages around him and felt there was more he could do than just assist in the clinic. One day he felt a strong urge to walk through Respuesta Sociale and pray for people in need. He meandered along the dusty roads, sidestepping the grunting pigs and cackling chickens that vied for scraps of food from the garbage piles. He knocked on dilapidated tar paper doors that offered a semblance of privacy for the tiny hovels. He stopped to talk to women preparing meals over their smoky outdoor cooking fires. Whenever possible he laid hands on the sick or downcast and asked God to heal them.

One young child was burning with fever. His dry, scaly skin had a sickly yellow tinge, his liver was enlarged and he was obviously jaundiced. He was listless and barely responsive and his condition was slowly deteriorating. Ian prayed for healing, realizing that humanly speaking there was nothing he could do – the child was dying.

The following day, the child's mother bounced into the clinic looking for Ian. Behind her scampered a healthy normal looking child. 'My child is well. It's a miracle!' she called excitedly to all who would listen. It was amazing. Ian could not believe this was the same moribund child he had examined the day before. The child's skin glowed pink and healthy, and his dark brown eyes sparkled with life. From our perspective, this really was a miracle, and we praised and thanked God for his intervention in this situation.

Talma listened to the story of the child's recovery with amazement. She was deeply touched by this incredible evidence of God's caring heart. Soon after, she dedicated her life to Christ and enthusiastically took on the position of chief evangelist for the clinic. Talma was transformed by her new found faith. She began holding Bible studies in her home. Her face, once so hard and bitter, now reflected love and gentleness. She wanted all the villagers to know that her life had been transformed and theirs could be also.

The impact of our dental team spread far beyond the filling of teeth to the changing of lives.

The last of the teams attached to the medical department was a small dedicated team of doctors and nurses who provided curative medical care. Jean Tomblin, a sandy haired nurse from Colorado, efficiently organized this group. She spent hours down in the hold searching for medications and supplies to cure the medical conditions they constantly met with in the villages. Sometimes this team worked alongside the dental team, treating ear infections, dosing children for worms and handing out vitamins. A steady stream of patients appeared from surrounding villages, often desperate for help.

On other occasions they visited the local prison and listened helplessly to the tragic stories many of the inmates told. They treated venereal disease and cautiously examined open sores that carried who-knew-what infections. They braved the unrest and possibility of violence, touched with compassion by the loneliness and hopelessness around them. The evangelism teams visited too. Prisoners listened avidly to the story of a God who really cared for their spiritual and physical condition. Soon inmates became Christians and before we left, a Bible study was under way each week. Once again, the power of God's love expressed through tangible physical aid had contributed to the revelation of a God who cares for every aspect of our lives.

Throughout this outreach, I struggled with how paltry our assistance seemed to be in comparison to the need. As news of the ship's visit spread, desperate people arrived from all over Mexico. Each morning a line of hopeful patients waited at the bottom of the gangway pleading for help. Sadly, our operating lists were already full to overflowing. We were forced to turn them away to trudge back over the weary miles to their homes. It was hard to pray and send such people on their way again. We all felt overwhelmed by the enormous need around us and frustrated by our inability to respond.

Statistically I realized, no matter how efficient the ship became, our efforts would never make any difference to the incidence of cleft lip and palates. Nor would they measurably impact the health care provision of Mexico. Yet in God's eyes what we were doing was very important because it expressed his love to people in need.

The words from Mt 25:40 flashed through my mind as I contemplated this problem. 'Whatever you did for one of the least of these brothers of mine, you did for me.' We are not called to change statistics, we are called to change lives, I realized. Each time we transformed a face, dressed a wound, relieved a painful toothache, or prayed for healing, we did so in the name of God. Our actions demonstrated the love and compassion of a God who cares deeply and passionately for each person he created.

Concentrating on the unfinished task would not help, I concluded. The overwhelming needs around us must never discourage our efforts. God asks us to energetically pour out our lives in whatever small way we are able to. As long as we do all we are capable of to reach out with his love and compassion we are fulfilling what he asks of us. Alone, our efforts look small, but working in co-operation with God, our lives can make an incredible difference in this world.

At the same time in the midst of these difficult and challenging experiences our lives were changed and enriched. We were more and more aware of how much we had to learn from these people we came to serve. Their different value systems, their courage and joyful acceptance in the face of adversity were all challenges to our faith and our way of life.

Chapter 12

HAVE STETHOSCOPE, WILL TRAVEL

> Those who go down to the sea in ships, who do business on
> great waters, they see the works of the Lord, and His wonders
> in the deep.
>
> Ps 107:23–24

I stood outside the Presbyterian church in Tema, Ghana, my heart aching. A sea of black faces – over a thousand. Desperate people milled around in front of me. Children with gaping holes in their faces huddled close to their mothers. Young adults, with tumours the size of melons protruding from their jaws, gazed toward me pleadingly. Old people with wizened faces and sightless cloudy eyes stared vacantly ahead. Many had trekked from hundreds of miles away. Some had slept in the church overnight, hoping to be first in line. All were waiting for the medical team of the *Anastasis* to examine them, hoping against hope that an operation would transform their faces, relieve their suffering, and renew their lives.

Tears sprang to my eyes as I watched one little four-year-old boy, his face half-eaten away by a skin infection. His jaw and teeth protruded through the gaping wound on the side of his face. Once it would have responded to a five-day course of antibiotics. Now he needed extensive surgery and skin grafting. Even then his appearance would never be fully restored.

Dr Gary stood at the door of his screening room wearily surveying the crowd. He had already examined dozens of patients and the numbers around him were still enormous. He was making some agonizing decisions, trying to decide whom he could best help. 'Keep this one, and this one,' he ordered. 'Send those ones home.' One man with an enormous tumour bulging out of the side of his face, wouldn't budge. 'I'm not moving until you do something for me,' he explained grimly.

Out in the middle of the room I watched Becky Bynum, a fair haired nurse from Houston, scurrying determinedly through the crowd. Her green surgical scrub outfit with its bright floral cuffs stood out conspicuously. Her hair was tied in a pony tail against the heat. Usually Becky had a bright smile for every child, but today tears ran down her face. She couldn't bear to turn the infants away and hunted for babies in the mass of crippled bodies. She snuck them into Gary's line, afraid that the schedule would be full before he saw them and they would miss out on an operation.

Dr Bob Dyer was hard at work on the other side of the enclosure. Quickly he passed down the ragged line of hopeful patients. The queue stretched like an endless tail away from his screening area. Prospective patients pressed closely around him as he shone a light in the eyes raised anxiously upward for him to examine. He too had to make hard and painful choices as to whom he could best help.

In a room off to one side sat those approved for operation. Their ravaged faces were aglow with new hope. Dr Felicity Cooper from England was performing physical examinations on them. Her stethoscope dangled around her neck and she firmly clasped her auroscope in one hand. She too was in tears, and would be throughout the whole of her three weeks on board. This was Felicity's first visit to Africa and the impact of the need around her was overpowering.

Next door, the lab staff was drawing blood. Babies screamed, centrifuges whirred, harassed and exhausted staff worked diligently to check patients' condition before surgery.

Not far away, the *Anastasis* evangelism team was also hard at work. They prayed with the patients Bob and Gary could not operate on. Lovingly and compassionately, they shared the story of a God who cared for each of his children in the midst of their pain and suffering. Many of the people clung to them and their message of hope, eagerly bowing their heads for this unexpected blessing.

This is just one example of the dramatic changes our lives underwent after that first outreach in Mexico with its meagre thirty-five prospective patients. Suddenly we were no longer just a ship with a mission, we were a ship with a story – a story of concern for the poor and care for the dispossessed.

We proudly told that story in many ports throughout the US, Canada and Europe in the following years, gathering new stories as we sailed from outreach to outreach. Jamaica, the Dominican Republic, Ghana, Togo, Guinea, the Ivory Coast, Lithuania, Estonia and others have all embraced the ministry of what is now the largest privately run hospital ship in the world.

In Portland, Oregon, on our return from Mexico in 1987 I felt I could almost hear the trumpets heralding our arrival. Fire boats, their hoses gushing forth towering fountains of water in a spectacular display, preceded us as we steamed up the river. We passed under the myriad of tightly-packed bridges that opened majestically as the *Anastasis* approached. Tugs nudged expertly at our sides, guiding us gently through the narrow passageways under the bridges and alongside the Boardwalk. This would be our berth for the next three weeks. Church groups, civic and professional leaders invaded the ship eager to hear about our adventures. Our medical reception filled to overflowing. Doctors, nurses, dentists and allied health professionals eagerly came on board to hear about the life-changing surgeries we had just performed in Mexico.

In Port Albernie, British Colombia, we wrinkled our noses at the smell of the adjacent paper pulp mill. It didn't deter the crowds that swarmed aboard. Many were challenged as never before by the needs of those so much less fortunate than themselves.

In Seattle, Washington, we occupied an old pier at the bottom of the Pike Place Market. From here we watched the ferries plying their way back and forth across the sparkling blue harbour to the snow-capped Olympic Peninsular. Tom Sine, tall and striking, with a humorous sparkle in his blue green eyes came on board. He had spent several years working with a project in Haiti. Now he was deeply committed to helping those less fortunate than ourselves. He brought a team from World Concern, a locally-based Christian organization, with him, hoping to initiate a networking relationship. World Concern generously offered medical supplies from their warehouse to supplement our depleted stores. Over the next few years they continued to supply us with much needed items. It was wonderful to network with others actively involved in ministry to the poor.

Tom, whom I married in 1992 shortly after I left the *Anastasis*, also initiated some other forms of networking during our visit. The next day, he chauffeured me around Seattle, excitedly sharing his favourite city and many of his ideas with his visitor who was somewhat distracted by thoughts of the upcoming outreach. We admired the breathtaking view across Seattle and its harbour towards the mountains on the peninsula. We drove around the beautiful university campus. We ate lunch interspersed with a diet of books and shared concerns for the poor and dispossessed. Sadly I waved goodbye as the ship left port, doubting that our rather hectic paths would ever cross again.

Sailing down the coast to Santa Cruz, California, the *Anastasis* anchored half a mile off shore and we hired launches to ferry tour groups on board. One enterprising young man decided to swim out for a visit. He arrived blue and shivering at our gangway suffering severely from hypothermia. Fortunately a hot bath soon revived him and he returned to shore by the more conventional method.

In Los Angeles we loaded our supplies from the port office, ready for another trip to Lazaro Cardenas. From there we sailed onward through the Panama Canal again and up to the East Coast of the US, preparing for ministry in the Caribbean Basin. Outreaches in Jamaica, and the Dominican Republic followed over the next few years. Eventually, the *Anastasis* steamed across the Atlantic once more to the ports of Europe and ministry opportunities in West Africa and Eastern Europe.

Glasgow, Scotland, was our first port of call in Europe. From there I dashed across the narrow country to the beautiful city of Edinburgh. From here my mother's family migrated to Australia in the early 1900s. I excitedly explored another part of my heritage, wandering in awe through this magnificent, historic city, with its colourful but turbulent past. I visited the mighty fortress of Edinburgh castle that sits perched high above the city on the sheer cliffs of Castle Rock. I walked down the Royal Mile past monuments and enticing historic sites to the splendid royal palace of Holyrood. I wandered the ancient twisting alleys, dark sombre lanes and cobbled thoroughfares of the Old Town intrigued by this city in which my forebears dwelt.

None of these splendid sights, however, could compare to the wonder of what was happening on the ship itself. From those spartan beginnings in Mexico, the medical and dental ministry expanded rapidly as we swept from port to port. To that one small operating room we soon added two more. On subsequent outreaches we performed orthopaedic, ENT and gynaecological surgery as well as maxillo-facial and ophthalmic surgery. Our ward, still with its old army stretchers squeezed together, expanded to hold twenty to thirty patients. The dental ministry grew to six portable units. The community health team enlarged to involve preventative as well as curative work. Flannelgraphs and posters helped teach basic health and hygiene to mothers and health advisers in villages and communities.

Then came some unexpected and exciting additions. Paul Moehring, a quiet, retiring dental technician from San Antonio, Texas, joined the crew to make dental bridges and crowns. We allocated him a tiny five feet by eight feet room at the bow of the ship. He crammed in grinding wheels, ovens and other marvellous paraphernalia, including the most sophisticated stereo system on the ship. The melodic strains of Mozart and Tchaikovsky resounded down the corridors as Paul worked. Sets of artificial teeth leered down from the shelves. Soon they were joined by prosthetic models for Gary's jaw operations, then by artificial eyes, ears and noses. These prostheses transformed faces as truly and impressively as any operation. Today, in his quiet unassuming way, Paul is working at the International Home Office in Texas. He is working to establish a unit for manufacturing artificial legs for amputees.

Paul is an incredible trophy of God's grace. Before his conversion to Christianity, he was involved with motorcycle gangs and criminal activities. Today he is transformed. Under his gruff exterior is a man with a deep, thoughtful faith and a rich understanding of the God whose love reached down and touched him in his moment of need. His life is now extended to helping not hurting others. Through Paul's vision we are seeing those words of Isaiah 35: 'Then will the lame leap like a deer' fulfilled in ways none of us had ever considered possible.

The medical staff also grew as the ministry moved into high gear. Today there are thirty medical and dental personnel working long-term on the *Anastasis*. Several more are busily employed at the administrative offices in Lindale, Texas, and Rotterdam, Holland, recruiting short-term volunteers, and organizing donations of supplies. With the addition of short- term volunteers, each time the ship pulled into a port in Mexico, Africa or the Caribbean, I suddenly found myself responsible for a team of over a hundred people.

Other aspects of the *Anastasis* ministry have grown too. Development teams organized sanitation schemes, launched agricultural projects and built structures from simple latrines to schools and hospital clinics. Evangelism teams often worked alongside the practical projects praying for families, establishing Bible studies and performing dramas representing the gospel story. Or they worked with local churches, evangelizing on the streets, in market places and in prisons.

And now there are other ships joined to the burgeoning Mercy Ships' fleet. The *Good Samaritan* (later renamed the *Island Mercy*) with its staff of sixty personnel, is ideal for mobile teams. Two dental units and teams of eager medical workers have made it possible for us to perform outreaches in Jamaica, Haiti, and several Central American countries. Now, the *Island Mercy* is busily at work in the South Pacific Islands.

In New Zealand, the *Pacific Ruby*, a luxury motor launch with space for only thirty persons, was donated. Presently, it is directed by David and Linda Cowie, those wonderful friends who first introduced me to Mercy Ships back in 1979. Along with the *Island Mercy*, the *Pacific Ruby* operates from a home base in Tauranga, New Zealand.

Much to my delight we were able to recruit Dr

Andrew Clark, a young enthusiastic New Zealand physician, who works part-time in private practice, to head up this part of the programme. I first met Andrew when I spoke to a group of medical students at Otago University in Dunedin back in 1983. To my amazement, for years he remembered and received encouragement from the words I shared with him concerning our need for patience as we work with our God to prepare for ministry. Now, under his direction, teams work throughout the South Pacific, including the islands of Tonga, Western Samoa and Vanuatu providing care facilities in optometry, dentistry and basic health care.

Lastly, in 1994, the *Caribbean Mercy* was acquired in Norway. It is already working in evangelism, medical and development work, and will soon be outfitted with a small ophthalmic clinic. It will continue the important work begun by the *Anastasis* and *Good Samaritan* in the Americas and Caribbean basin.

From the moment that first surgery was performed on board, my life too was transformed. The backwaters of Greece, the doubts and frustrations of Hawaii, and the chilling sense of being in the graveyard, were all behind me. It truly seemed that this was what I had come into medicine for, and I was happier, more satisfied and more fulfilled than I had ever thought possible. I moved from ship to shore team, from vessel to vessel, and back to the land bases, directing procedures, helping solve problems and drinking in the results of this incredible ministry. The images of those days are indelibly etched on my mind.

For example, in Barahona in the Dominican Republic, the *Anastasis* berthed at the end of the main street. Her white hull and commanding presence dominated the small town. Everybody heard about the great ship with its surgeons on board. The news of medical, and construction teams spread rapidly throughout the surrounding countryside.

Little Arturo came to us with his mouth almost welded shut as a result of chemical burns. He sat alone on the metal steps outside the ward eating his dinner, greatly embarrassed by his shameful situation. In order to eat, he rubbed food up his face with his hand. This forced it through the tiny hole in the front of his teeth. Gary assisted one of our visiting surgeons to slit the tissue binding his lips. They gave him a new mouth. He left the ship singing and grinning and using his face like any normal little boy.

Then there was Juanita, a five-year-old girl with burns and contractures under her chin. She was a little imp of a girl with dark mischievous eyes and short black frizzy hair. Unfortunately news came to her slowly in her isolated village. She appeared on the last day of our first trip to the Dominican Republic. It was too late to do anything. Becky Bynum was deeply touched by her plight and prayed for her regularly over the next few months.

On our next visit, Becky hunted around Santo Domingo for the child, praying fervently she would be able to find her. She asked every patient who came for screening if they knew Juanita. She wandered the streets describing the little girl and trying to locate her. But to no avail. No one knew who Juanita was and Becky returned to the ship in Barahona dispirited and disheartened.

As she dragged her exhausted body from the van to the gangway, Becky stopped and gasped in amazement. There, standing waiting for her, a broad grin from ear to ear, was little Juanita. Becky raced over and hugged her. Then she grabbed Dr Gary and insisted he see the child. Soon Juanita was scheduled for surgery. Becky rejoiced. God had answered her prayers.

We made a neck brace for Juanita to wear after her operation. This stopped the contractures from re-occurring. It was tied with bright multi-coloured shoelaces over her head. The assortment of little bows contrasted vividly with her black frizzy hair and white hospital gown, covered in its assortment of small animal designs. She wore them proudly round the ward for days, then left the ship to return to her village and parade them to her family and friends.

Becky loved children and they were as attracted to her as to a pied piper. Sometimes, however, there were a few too many even for her to deal with. One evening as she looked over the operating list for the next day, Becky realized with dismay that there were six small infants to be admitted – and she only had three cribs available. She urgently called the carpentry department. 'Can you make my beds into two?' was her startling request. The carpenters promptly arrived with wooden partitions and divided the cots.

That night the ward bulged at the seams. Thirty-seven patients, twenty-nine of them less than five years of age, crowded with their families into our forty foot long ward. Screaming babies and whimpering, confused toddlers, vied with their shouting anxious parents for attention from the harassed staff. Lab technicians arrived to draw blood. They waded through the wall-to-wall bodies endeavouring to find the right patient. Sweaty unclean bodies added their odiferous aroma to the claustrophobic atmosphere of the tiny ward. Unfortunately there was no shower available. The air-conditioner worked overtime, unable to cope with the overwhelming load.

Finally everyone began to settle down for the night. Some lay on the tiled floor under the cribs, trying to draw comfort from the cool surface. Others climbed into the stretchers, often trying to cram four people into our ancient rickety beds. These creaked and groaned under the unaccustomed weight. Sometimes the strain was just too much. The wooden legs cracked and the stretchers collapsed, spewing their load in all directions.

Miraculously, Becky and her nursing team somehow managed to organize the confusion and chaos. They washed tiny, squirming bodies in preparation for the day ahead, and decked them out in clean white hospital gowns. The lab staff laboured overtime long into the night, cross-matching blood and checking blood chemistry. By the next morning every patient was ready for surgery, but Becky had had her fill of babies for a while.

For me, life was full to overflowing. It was packed with new adventures, unusual challenges and an array of unexpected learning experiences. Sometimes the surprises were still disconcerting enough to make me want to pack up my bags and head for home. Amazingly, it was often the little things that most upset my equilibrium.

While the *Anastasis* was in Jamaica, for example, I decided it was time to renovate my cabin. Apart from the addition of the cabinets my church had graciously provided in New Zealand, it had hardly been altered in the forty years since the ship was built and was desperately in need of an overhaul. The grey vinyl bulkheads were still scarred and dilapidated from the sprinkler system days, and my narrow bunk had become more and more uncomfortable. I planned to rip out the upper bunk, tear out part of the bulkhead and install a hideaway bed that would fold into the wall. This would give me a small living space during the daytime. I was sick of sitting on my bed and wanted room to install a comfortable, reclining chair.

As with all renovations on the *Anastasis*, the task was far more complex than we anticipated. In order to tear out the bulkhead, we needed to remove a light fixture. This meant pulling down the overhead yet again, in order to work on the electrical system. That involved turning off the sprinkler system temporarily in order to remove the sprinkler head.

The plumber stopped at the local valve station and confidently turned off what he thought was the section supplying my cabin. He reached up to unscrew the sprinkler head and gasped in horror as black sludge blasted out from behind his hand. Freed from its narrow restricting pipe, the highly pressurized stream gushed out exuberantly, deluging my unsuspecting cabin. It aimed straight for my sheepskin coat hanging behind the door. It splattered my bedspread with black putrid sludge, splotching and soaking the clean washing I had just placed on it.

The plumber fought desperately to replace the cap, realizing that he had turned off the wrong circuit. Alas, the pressure was too great. Behind the black sludge came a torrent of water that cascaded across the cabin and out of the door. In a panic he raced back to the valve station, now unsure which circuit he needed to disconnect. The water raced behind him, flooding its way down the hallway and into the adjacent cabins. People erected barricades to divert it away from their belongings.

It was almost an hour before the right valve was turned off and the flood subsided. My friends and I hovered at the doorway to my cabin stunned by the disaster within. A layer of smelly, black sludge clung tenaciously to everything in sight. It had sat for months in those pipes growing fouler and more fetid as it stewed and stagnated in the confined space. Now it dripped from the bulkheads and oozed into the bottom of my closets. My clothes hung in a sodden mess and my sheepskin coat, which had protected me through so many bitterly cold days in Victoria, was a black unrecognizable bundle.

Amazingly, even this horrific event had a silver lining. My church in New Zealand, hearing of my plight, sent me a brand new coat. Then, on our return to the US, a church in Houston, Texas, collected an offering. The pastor's wife escorted me on a shopping spree. Everything that had been destroyed was abundantly replaced and my cabin was soon sparkling like new. Fresh shiny floral wallpaper covered the black splotches on the bulkheads. New carpet adorned the deck and a beautiful beige, Danish style reclining chair stood in one corner. I could hardly believe the blessing God provided out of such a seeming disaster.

On another occasion, I returned to the ship after a trip to the International Home Office, exhausted and bedraggled by my travels. By now I was paranoid about the fact that while I was away, cockroaches often bred in the drains below my cabin. The moment I arrived, I vigorously embarked on my usual cockroach eradication procedure. I entered the bathroom and nervously shook the towels and shower curtain looking for lurking insects. I flushed hot water down the drains and awaited the emergence of my dreaded enemies. I opened the cupboards and examined every surface to expose their hiding places. Then with a sigh of relief, I decided to have a shower. No sooner had I entered the shower stall than I felt something on my leg. I looked down, and there it was! A great big fat cockroach crawling up my leg. I jumped out and squashed it with my shoe. Then I stood trembling for a moment regaining my courage. Hesitantly I stepped back in, to finish my shower. No sooner had I grabbed the soap than another animal latched onto my leg. I don't think I have ever come closer to leaving the ship than at that moment.

Incidents such as these taught me that this kind of work required a lively sense of humour. Walking along God's pathway is always a risky, adventurous business. We never reach the point where we can relax and feel comfortable. This is particularly true when the direction of our life is geared toward helping those less fortunate than ourselves. In fact I was beginning to suspect that Christian living is not meant to be comfortable. When our lives are constantly relaxed and at ease, it is usually because we begin to water down what it really means to be a Christian.

I was never more aware of that than when I returned to the United States after being in an impoverished nation. On one occasion, I walked into a Christian bookstore and was appalled by the barrage of self-help and inwardly focused books on the shelves. The view of Christianity expressed in this store was entirely concerned with encouraging me to satisfy my own selfish needs. It was totally uninterested in assisting me to reach out and satisfy the needs of others.

Ministering to others is, I believe, is the true focus of our faith. The Christ we follow had nowhere to lay his head. He was never concerned for himself or his own comforts. His life was devoted to extending God's love to our world. His emphasis was healing the sick, feeding the hungry and preaching the Good News to the poor. As a Westerner from a very affluent and self-involved Christianity, I realized more and more how much I needed to discover the servant Christ in some new ways too.

Fortunately, our lives were not all hard work and no play. Many amusing incidents also occurred to lighten the strain. One particularly memorable occasion was the opportunity I had to participate in a medical outreach with the crew of the *Good Samaritan* on the island of La Gonaive, off the west coast of Haiti.

I flew into Port-au-Prince the day after an attempted coup. Soldiers in battle fatigues wandered the deserted streets with machine-guns slung over their shoulders. People hid fearfully in the tiny hovels that squatted close around the town, waiting for the violence and destruction to end.

We gladly left this restless city behind us and sped down the coast to St Marc, a small fishing port on the west coast. The *Good Samaritan* bobbed impatiently at anchor while we loaded our supplies. A quick trip transported us across the intervening strait to the island. Much to my relief, the sea was calm with hardly a ripple of discomfort. The water shone like a mirror and sunshine danced warmly off the calm blue surface. I had once vowed and declared I would never sail on the *Good Samaritan*. I had been told she would roll on anything – even wet grass.

The ship drew in toward the coastline. We anchored several hundred feet off shore, close to a narrow passageway in the reef that surrounded La Gonaive. Piles of boxes were disgorged into a small battered launch and hurried ashore. There were tents and kitchen utensils, medical supplies and food. Our target was a village two hours walk up a rough mountain path. We carried with us all the paraphernalia necessary to set up a permanent camp for the duration of our stay.

I clambered up the track, feeling wet and sticky in the tropical heat. My companions included the *Good Samaritan's* directors, Jack and Cherie Minton and their two teenage children, Tiffany and Philip. Jack is a born comedian. His black moustache twitched mischievously as he enlivened our tedious walk with constant jokes and comedy performances.

We trudged up the dry barren path, past tumbledown mud huts and dry spindly vegetation. We staggered past villagers stooped over enormous piles of smouldering wood. These burned slowly to produce charcoal for cooking fires. The constant search for fuel was devastating the landscape. A swarm of ragged dirty children soon clung to us like magnets. They chattered excitedly at the strange white band of foreigners sweating their way slowly past their homes. We were the best entertainment they had seen for months.

Then we crested the hill and gazed in astonishment at the unusual campsite. A circle of grey and red dome tents sprouted from the landscape like mushrooms from some alien planet. They were just big enough for three sleeping pads. In one corner of the enclosure, two small, black plastic-shrouded stalls stood out conspicuously. They housed our latrine and shower. In another corner stood a large open-air tent surrounded by mosquito nets. It housed our kitchen and food supplies. Relaxing in the shade sat our team members. Some were praying. Others strummed guitars and sang. A rope stretched tautly through the brush marked the perimeter of our camp. It kept at bay the inquisitive locals who stood and stared for hours puzzling over our strange customs. In the distance we could hear the eerie voodoo chants.

Our clinic was established in an old concrete school building that stood dark and damp at the edge of the village. The single large room was divided into pharmacy, examining rooms and waiting areas. The doctors often emerged from its dim recesses to examine patients outside in the brilliant sunshine. They peered into ears and eyes and mouths, diagnosing infections, prescribing pills, ministering care. In the afternoon an evangelism team performed dramas in a nearby clearing. Their painted faces and brightly coloured costumes attracted an eager crowd of onlookers. One young child clung to the branches of a tree in order to see. He reminded me of Zaccheus eager to listen to the stories of Jesus.

It was the trip back to the ship that was particularly memorable. In a somewhat misguided effort to be helpful, our local organizers hired donkeys for us to ride. We inspected their wooden saddles and bony uncomfortable backs in horror. Dressed as I was in a white skirt and blue tee shirt, I had little desire to mount such a smelly animal but didn't want to offend our friends. Cherie, Jack and I mounted awkwardly, surrounded by a laughing crowd of willing assistants. The animals brayed nervously and sidled back and forth as we tried to control them. They clearly sensed our inexperience.

Slowly we manoeuvred down the trail, laughing and joking as we went. The donkeys were small, and Jack's feet almost dragged on the ground. Our puzzled child guides followed behind on their own beasts, swishing at the rumps of our donkeys with whips to keep them moving. They couldn't understand our feeble attempts to direct the donkeys. For them it was as simple as walking.

At the bottom of the hill, large muddy patches stretched out toward the wharf. A rainstorm had just swept through the area, freshening the air, but making our progress hazardous. By now we were all laughing uproariously at Jack's constant jokes and our own comical antics. Our donkeys definitely had minds of their own, and took full advantage of our inexperience. They stopped suddenly for a rest then stubbornly refuse to budge. No amount of coaxing would change their minds. Then suddenly they decided we were moving too slowly. They broke into a canter accompanied by our anxious screams as we clung precariously to the saddles.

The slippery, slidey mud provided new adventures we had never imagined. It clung tenaciously to the animals' hooves and splattered our dangling ankles. The donkeys slipped and slid across the shiny surface seeking desperately for firm footholds on the treacherous expanse. Then suddenly in unison, both Cherie's and my animal plopped to the ground. Their legs splayed out awkwardly at right angles and we were dumped in a laughing heap into the welcoming mud. We jumped off as the mud sucked hungrily at our legs and shoes and staggered away. Our braying, struggling mounts thrashed around helplessly trying to right themselves. Jack shouted quips and comments from a safe distance unwilling to join our muddy party. Cherie and I had had enough. We continued our slipping, sliding journey on foot, much to the relief of the distressed animals.

Unfortunately, not all the memories are as carefree and hilarious as this one. There were others that pulled strongly at my heart strings and remoulded my faith as I continued to learn from my sisters and brothers in the developing world.

One of my most vivid and tragic memories was of the malnourished children often brought to the screening sessions. This pulled at all of our hearts. On one occasion, a small slender woman in a ragged purple dress hesitantly handed Dr Gary Parker a tiny bundle. Inside the dirty blanket lay a poor skeleton of child with a severe cleft lip and palate. Little Wanda was six weeks old. She couldn't suck properly and was grossly malnourished. As well as that, in her attempts to take in life-giving fluids, she had inhaled milk into her lungs. Her emaciated little body gasped painfully for air. Her tiny chest heaved in and out with the strain imposed by the pneumonic infection that was overwhelming her lungs.

What a pitiful heart-rending sight. The chances of saving her were slim but we wanted to try. Gary radioed the ship and we hurried her onto the *Anastasis* and down to the hospital.

We anxiously inserted a nasogastric tube past the gap in Wanda's palate and pushed nourishing fluids into her body. A wide strip of white tape secured the tube to her nose. It dwarfed her fragile, tiny face and emaciated little body. She was cold and shivery in spite of the hot humid air, and we found a white woollen hat for her head. It was far too big and kept falling over her eyes. We shrouded her in warm towels and watched as she nestled into the sheepskin rug beneath her for extra warmth.

The medical staff all hovered around Wanda anxious to will her back to life. We all wished we personally could draw each painful breath into her poor tortured body and take the agony from her.

Sadly, it was already too late for little Wanda. She died forty-eight hours later, surrounded by her family and the grieving medical staff.

It was the reaction of Wanda's mother, Iris, that most challenged us. She accepted the inevitability of Wanda's death long before we did. She embraced it willingly as part of the framework of the world in which she lived.

For us, trained in our sophisticated medical world there was less acceptance. For us, there was an overarching sense of failure. Our medical training had proved inadequate, and our prayers for healing went unanswered. Sadly, we transferred our sense of failure to God. We questioned the reasonableness of God who not only allowed such suffering but who refused to heal when we wanted him to. It was as though we expected God to react like a puppet on a string. We wanted him to respond to our unreasonable demands when and how we asked.

This incident was the beginning of yet another Bible search for me. 'Why does God allow suffering?' I wanted to know. 'Where does death fit into his purposes?' This became yet another aspect of God's expanding educational project for my struggling Christian life. Again it would be a long time before I was aware of the answers but in Iris's response I glimpsed some of them.

Incredibly, Wanda's death was a time of new life and strengthening faith for her mother, Iris. The staff prayed with Iris throughout her ordeal. After Wanda's death they helped her with funeral arrangements and formed part of the grieving crowd following the tiny coffin to its grave. Afterwards, some of the nurses visited Iris's humble abode, a small wooden hut high on the hill, with banana thatched roof and tiny shuttered windows. It was easy to find. You turned right where the little old lady constantly sat over her fire and then turned left at the pig that always seemed to obstruct the road.

The nurses brought gifts of baby formula for Wanda's twin brother. He was also malnourished and Iris accepted the provisions gratefully. However, much to our amazement, Iris did not keep this unexpected windfall for herself. She shared it with the neighbourhood mothers, humbling us with her generous spirit and open-handed attitude to our gifts.

With the encouragement of one of the ship's nurses, Deidre Vanzant, Iris soon began Bible studies in her home. She raided the surrounding dwellings each week, borrowing their meagre furniture. She set up a circle of twelve chairs for ship friends and neighbours. Together they studied the gospels, reflecting on the significance of Christ and his teachings in their own lives.

Over the next few weeks we watched Iris change. Her face began to radiate new hope and her countenance glowed with a new inner light. Life would never be easy for her. Her husband had deserted her. She had little means of support. But amazingly, as she studied the Bible, she seemed to gain a confidence that God would look after her. Her simple faith, in the light of a hard and uncompromising existence, challenged our own faith that so often rocked under the impact of far less difficult circumstances.

It was Iris's incredible acceptance of the pain and suffering and the miracle of new life in her life that taught me the most during this difficult episode. It helped me tremendously in my struggle to understand the broader dimensions of suffering and our need to embrace it in the same way we accepted the idea of healing.

For me this struggle came to a height when the ship was in the Cote d'Ivoire, on the west coast of Africa. One of the patients Dr Gary screened for surgery was a little two-year-old boy, Mobio Bienvenue. Mobio had a large rubbery tumour, the size of a grapefruit, protruding grotesquely from his neck. It had been growing rapidly for three months and Gary feared it was a highly malignant tumour. We took a biopsy and asked the boy's mother to bring him back in a couple of weeks. Then we prayed. We did not really expect anything dramatic to happen, but were convinced none the less that prayer was an important element of all we did.

Two weeks later, Gary spied the boy's mother, a committed animist, down in the ward. He wasn't looking forward to the interview. The biopsy had confirmed his worst fears. The tumour was a highly malignant cancer.

Mobio's mother grinned broadly at Gary as he

hunted round the room for a child with an enormous tumour. Suddenly he realized that Mobio was tugging at his leg. He gazed down in shock at the totally normal child beaming up at him. The tumour had totally disappeared. As Gary examined Mobio's body he could find no evidence of any abnormal masses. But he wasn't convinced. He asked the child to return in another two weeks, then another, then another, until the end of the outreach. His face remained smooth and normal. Mobio's healing seemed complete. It really was a miracle.

The only one who wasn't surprised was the boy's mother. After all, we had prayed in Jesus' name hadn't we? If our God was really as powerful as we believed why all the fuss? Of course he would heal her son.

A few days after we first examined Mobio, another child with a huge tumour came to the screening session. Little Koyo Doho was three years old and obviously in great pain. Her eye bulged in a huge unsightly mass from its socket. Little Koyo was also prayed for. Sadly her eye did not respond and no miracle occurred in response to our prayers. When she returned a couple of weeks later, her suffering had increased and she was obviously about to die. There was nothing we could do to ease her agony.

Healing and suffering are both mysteries that all of us have to wrestle with in some form or other. We recognize that health and healing is God's desire rather than sickness and disease, but this often makes the struggle even more difficult. There are certainly no simple answers. Interestingly in the early church, healing and health were closely linked to an acceptance of suffering as an identification with the sufferings of Christ. An understanding of physical illness and the existence of suffering were closely associated with healing. They were all seen as part of a larger paradigm in which God's grace works through human weakness.

As well as the challenges from my brothers and sisters in developing nations, I am indebted to the Mennonite church and their struggle to interpret this complex topic for much of my growing understanding in this area. I have also learned much from wonderful books such as Francis MacNutt's *Healing*[2] and the MARC publication *Health, Healing and Transformation*[3].

As Francis MacNutt affirms, 'God has revealed himself as being on the side of life, of wholeness, of health in spirit, mind and body.' The whole message of Christ in the New Testament, as he healed the sick, raised the dead and fed the hungry proclaims that.

I believe that sickness has no place in God's new Kingdom. Rev 21:4 with its imagery of the totally fulfilled Kingdom of God is of tremendous encouragement to me here. As I work amongst the suffering in our world, I long for that day on which 'He will wipe every tear from their eyes. There will be no more death or mourning or crying or pain, for the old order of things has passed away.' We are called as followers of Christ to be ministers of physical healing just as much as we are of spiritual healing. In the Bible there is no distinction. The words translated 'salvation' and 'healing' in the New Testament come from the same root word. 'Salvation, in the context of sin, is the restoration to wholeness of that which is fragmented, the healing of that which is damaged and the health of that which is subject to sickness, decay and death'[4].

Yet in the midst of salvation and healing, we must still contend with death, disease and suffering, both on the physical and spiritual level. Many of us know the pain of praying for those we love and seeing no change occur. Others have experienced miraculous and instantaneous answers to their prayers for loved ones. None of us understand why.

So it is with our prayers for physical healing. Sometimes the answers are instant and miraculous. Sometimes they take much hard work and physical effort on our part, as in the performance of surgery. At other times we see no change at all, or disaster of disasters, the patient dies.

I believe that both healing and suffering are intimately linked through the Cross. It is the Cross and Christ's redemptive work on it that is the power to heal in our world. At the same time, it is the greatest symbol of suffering that we can imagine. Christ endured unimaginable pain and agony in order to set God's creation free from all that bound and corrupted it. There is no doubt in my mind that sickness is evil and is not directly willed by God. It is a result of the fall of humankind, and of the sin and evil that still exist in our world. Because of that, people continue to suffer and to die and will do so, as little Koyo did, until God's Kingdom is revealed in all its glory and fullness.

There are other dimensions too, in suffering. It may have a higher purpose in our own lives personally. As many of us know, God does work through illness to chastise us or bring us to our senses.

Probably the least understood and most confusing aspect of suffering is that of 'redemptive suffering', where Christ asks us to share in his sufferings as a special privilege in identifying with him and his suffering on the Cross. In Phil 3:10-11 Paul says 'I want to know Christ and the power of his resurrection and the fellowship of sharing in his sufferings, becoming like him in his death, and so, somehow, to attain to the resurrection from the dead.'

In this framework we are also called to identify with the sufferings of others in our world, to share their pain and to weep with their tears. Our own sufferings can create a strong and solid foundation from which we are able to reach out with love and compassion to a wounded world. As Paul affirms in 2 Cor 1:5 'For just as the sufferings of Christ flow over into our lives, so also through Christ our comfort overflows.' And it is through our compassion that we reveal our loving, caring God to the world. Even more miraculous than any of the physical miracles God performs, I believe that each time we pray for the sick, give sight to the blind, and make the lame leap like a deer, we are catching the first glimpses of that new heaven and new earth without death or disease or pain or suffering, so joyously promised in Revelation 21.

Chapter 13

A MIXED MULTITUDE

All nations will come and worship before you, For your right-
eous acts have been revealed.

Rev 15:4

Sunshine danced off the warm tropical waters.
Seagulls screeched overhead. Giant cranes like enormous metal giraffes silhouetted the skyline. They
moved slowly along the waterfront depositing their
heavy loads of cargo containers in long lines awaiting
Customs inspection. Black smoke belched from the
adjacent industrial area contributing a grey haze to
the vivid blue sky.

Tugs bustled alongside and manoeuvred the big
white ship into what would be its berth for the next
three months. A rhythmic drum beat and the sound
of clapping hands reached the ears of the crew leaning excitedly over the ship's rails. Local Christians,
their supple bodies swaying gracefully back and
forth to the sound, praised God in a song and dance
welcome. The women dressed in intricately designed
batik dresses and matching turbans added bright
splashes of colour to the welcoming crowd.

This was Lome, the capital city of Togo, a narrow
strip of a country between Ghana and West Benin. It

was my third visit to West Africa, and the first for the *Anastasis*. Already I knew that it would be tough to shake this wondrous continent from my spirit. The rich and generous hospitality of the people and their exuberant fun-loving personalities were a constant delight.

Africa, four times larger than the United States, is as diverse and complex as it is huge. It is inhabited by over 2000 ethnic groups, most of which have their own specific language or dialect. There are the tall and proud Masai of East Africa and the tiny Pygmies of the Kalahari – with every possible variation between. Some live in hot, searing deserts and others in exotic rainforests or sweeping grasslands. They are nomads and agriculturalists, hunters and gatherers. Theirs is a rich and amazing heritage, extending back into the antiquity of time.

Lome, like most major African cities today, is an amazing contrast of old and new. Modern skyscrapers dominate the skyline. Black businessmen walk nonchalantly along the street in three-piece Western suits intermingled with their brothers in the striking African batik suits and long flowing gowns. On the outskirts squat the crowded mud and tin shacks of the shanty towns with their narrow dusty pathways and open sewers.

Close by is the traditional African market, the largest in West Africa. Tiny wooden booths squeeze closely together around a large concrete building. Their counters overflow with an incredible array of merchandise. Rows of tiny elephants and giraffes, beautifully carved in wood and ebony, sit quietly beside lions crouched ready to pounce. Strings of beads, red, blue and amber vie with woven bags of ochre, purple and black, for our attention. Above our heads dangle cool cotton shirts and skirts of bright yellow Kenti cloth or swirling batik designs. In the half light inside the concrete building we spy a sumptuous display of fruit and vegetables – pineapples and papaws (papayas), mangoes and custard apples beckon temptingly to us. The smell of blood from freshly killed animals mingles unpleasantly with the sweat and urine of the tightly pressed human occupants. Women with calabashes balanced expertly on their heads drive hard bargains for their daily shopping. On their backs they tote their ever-present babies, sleeping peacefully amidst the constant babble.

Outside the city, the country is flat and low-lying. The scrub-covered plains are dotted with scraggly thorn trees and sparse vegetation. The air smells strongly of goats and cattle as we drive our vehicles up the bumpy pot-holed road to the mud thatched huts of a rural village. We thankfully set up our medical clinic in the cool concrete school building shrouded by trees and shadow. Inside is a hive of activity. In one corner of the large room – a stethoscope dangling limply round his neck – sits a doctor interviewing patients. He listens intently to the translators interpreting symptoms over the babble of voices surrounding them. It isn't easy – one person translates from the local dialect to French and then another into English. A small curtained doorway behind them opens into a tiny suffocatingly hot examination room.

In another area, open boxes disgorge their assorted bottles of medications over a wooden table. The pharmacist pantomimes instructions at the patients to reinforce the interpreter's efforts. Close by, a nurse stands surrounded by a sea of bandaged bodies waiting for her attention. An old woman with a leg infection sits on a chair in front. The nurse cleanses the wound and applies a dressing. Off to one side in the waiting area patients sit on hard wooden benches, their eyes glued to the TV set. They are watching the film '*Jesus*', played in French, constantly commenting on the dialogue and listening intently as though to real people.

The press of bodies grew more and more hectic as news of our clinic spread. Swarms of villagers had wended their way along the narrow tracks from adjacent settlements. On the last day of our visit, frantic patients jostled wildly for a position in the queue that snaked its away around the village square. Our Togolese translators worked furiously – English to French to the local language – and then back again.

One helper spoke rapidly to a young woman with numerous strings of brightly coloured beads around her neck. His young face was intent and concerned. The woman was undecided between her faith in Christ and her trust in ancestral gods. The translator was suggesting she make a choice. Slowly she bowed her head in prayer acknowledging Christ. Suddenly one of her strands of beads broke. They bounced across the floor – bing, bing, bing. The translator grinned and praised God. The necklace that broke was a fetish, an animist charm, the only one she wore.

Just before lunch, an old grey haired man was carried in on a stretcher. He had fallen out of a tall tree, and now his scalp was bleeding and his chest flailed uselessly. His breath was weak and ragged. There was little we could do and we quickly sent him off to the hospital. Later we heard he died on the way.

The crowds around us continued to swell as the day progressed. One of the local villagers explained our sudden popularity. The man who died was the local witchdoctor and he was very jealous of our presence. On this particular day he had been out gathering leaves. He planned to make a fetish and cast a curse on us. His death convinced the people that our God was far stronger than his. It was an auspicious beginning to years of challenging ministry in many parts of West Africa.

From Togo, we sailed to Tema, Ghana, skirting the white sand beaches along the coast. On the shoreline, wooden dugout canoes and piles of fishing nets marked the tiny village settlements that had depended for centuries on the sea for their livelihood.

Proudly awaiting our arrival in Tema, their faces wreathed in smiles, stood Mary and Faithful Biney. Faithful, erect and proud in his light grey suit, watched excitedly as the tugs swung the ship portside to the dock. Beside him Mary firmly clutched little Donny, their four-year-old son. Her dark, slender figure looked very regal in a purple batik outfit with its long slim skirt and turban headdress. The material was covered with an intricate gold pattern that matched her flashing gold ear-rings. Esther, their ten-year-old daughter, waved eagerly from the ship's deck. She had sailed with the *Anastasis* from Togo. Her beautiful big, brown eyes sparkled with joy as she explored the huge white vessel that had been her home for the first few years of her life.

The Bineys first came to the *Anastasis* in 1980 when Faithful was a marine engineer and Mary a young blushing bride. Esther was born in Greece during those long hard days of preparation, which had as profound an impact on their lives as they did on mine. Together with the rest of the ship's community who participated in those difficult days in Greece, Mary and Faithful struggled with the challenges of establishing this new ministry. They too learned the importance of perseverance through hardship and the resulting joy of seeing a new ministry come into being.

Then they returned to Ghana, convinced God had called them to develop a ministry amongst their own people. Their time on board strengthened their faith. Now, both of them were zealous evangelists. They were convinced they could make a difference for God in their own country. As well as that, their hearts ached at the death and disease around them. They knew the pain of losing family in time of drought and friends to unnecessary disease. They wanted to establish agricultural projects and a medical clinic to care for the physical needs of their countrymen. In the restless and often turbulent environment of Ghana, they struggled against suspicion and misunderstanding to establish a Youth With A Mission base that was involved in both practical and spiritual ministry.

Over the years, Mary and Faithful continued to pray for the *Anastasis*. They hoped that one day the ship would visit their part of the world. The moment we started talking about Africa they pleaded with us to consider Ghana.

My first visit to Africa was spent in their home, a small concrete block abode, squashed into one of the many noisy suburban complexes around Tema. From the top of its flat roof I could survey the whole neighbourhood. Over the back fence, half a dozen black and white goats bleated plaintively in the tiny dirt enclosure. Next door a woman pounded away with a long heavy pole at a yellowish mass. She was making fufu, a local concoction of mashed plantain that was one of the staples of their diet. Across the dirt road, eroded with deep corrugated ruts, a man worked under a large shady tree. He was repairing motor bikes. Music blared late into the night and sounds echoed loudly round the concrete structures.

The house was hot and stuffy. It was often over-crowded with friends and visitors, but nothing could dim Mary and Faithful's enthusiasm. They worked tirelessly over the years to open doors for the *Anastasis's* visit to Ghana. And during that first visit to Africa, I reaped the benefits of their efforts. I was privileged to meet the President's wife, the Minister of Health and other important government officials. One official became very excited when I shared about the surgeries and construction work the *Anastasis* would perform. 'This is what Christianity is meant to be about,' he exclaimed. 'If more Christians worked like this, I might become a Christian too.'

Mary and Faithful are but a couple of the thousands of people whose lives have been radically transformed by time spent on board one of the Mercy Ships. Young and old, skilled and non-skilled, Europeans, Africans, Asians and Americans, so many have come and shared in our journey for a day, a year or a lifetime and never been the same. Each volunteer has made a unique contribution to the ministry that has not only transformed their own lives but those of thousands of others as well. I wish I could tell the stories of all who have worked on the Mercy Ships, unfortunately a few examples will have to suffice.

One person who has made a tremendous contribution to my own life as well as to the ministry of the *Anastasis*, is Simonne Dyer. She first joined Mercy Ships during the *Anastasis's* visit to her native land, New Zealand, when she was still Simonne McClusky. A slim grey haired woman in her early fifties, she had boundless energy and a deep desire to follow Christ. Initially, she worked at the port office in Auckland, New Zealand, then joined the ship's crew as Don Stephens' secretary. Simonne's wisdom and spiritual maturity were apparent to all who met her and it was no surprise to most of us when she became Don's assistant and then Chief Executive Officer of the *Anastasis*, in which role she still serves. In 1989, much to the delight of all the crew, Simonne married Dr Bob Dyer.

Simonne and I became close friends during that difficult sojourn in Honolulu. In the evenings we often took long walks together, discussing our spiritual state, the condition of the ministry and other serious topics as we strode vigorously through the streets. Occasionally our intense conversations were interrupted by cockroaches. Simonne hated them as much as I did and would race after them as they scampered along the footpaths, stomping enthusiastically and grinding them to dust under her feet.

Simonne was a wonderful role model for me as I struggled to develop the medical ministry. Her deep concern for all the crew, her strong leadership gifts and spiritual wisdom provided constant examples for me to follow.

On one occasion, the tremendous respect Simonne engendered amongst those she worked with created rather unexpected consequences. On the *Anastasis's* second visit to Ghana, the Chief of Tema sent a delegation to the ship dressed in the long flowing, traditional robes complete with gold chains and his staff of office. They invited her to his palace for a reception. Speaking in his native language of Ga, the Chief thanked Simonne for bringing the *Anastasis* to Ghana, then told her she looked like an old lady who had lived in his area for over 100 years. 'Thanks a lot Chief!' she thought. 'I don't think I look quite that old do I?' He then went on to explain that what he meant was that Simonne had the same spirit as this old lady and because of that he felt she was part of them. Therefore he had decided to make her the Queen Mother of the area.

Simonne was deeply touched by this unexpected honour and followed meekly as three old ladies took her into the palace and dressed her for the enstoolment – chiefs in Ghana sit on a stool, not a throne. She was wrapped in a rich royal robe with a knotted scarf tied around her head. Ceremonial sandals were put on her feet. Then, to the beating of drums, she was led to an ornately carved, white wooden stool decorated with the Knot of Wisdom and covered with a fringed, orange cushion. She was seated and raised three times and then proclaimed Naa (queen) Dede (firstborn girl).

For Simonne life continued as usual in spite of her new status. After all she still had to work, though the reasons for this needed to be explained to the Chief. He even wanted to send her servants to do her washing, cleaning and cooking. They were also to form part of her retinue whenever she went out.

Another memorable volunteer was Chief Ralph Niles. Ralph had spent a lifetime at sea, as an engineer. Now he was almost deaf and thought his seafaring days were over. However when the *Anastasis* sailed into San Francisco, this crusty old salt gave up his retirement plans in order to help. He and his wife Sarah spent many years serving on board both the *Anastasis* and the *Good Samaritan*.

I once asked Sarah what she thought about this. After all, she must have been looking forward to a peaceful retirement, comfortably established at home. 'It's the best thing that ever happened to us,' Sarah told me. 'I was watching Ralph grow old and forgetful in front of me. Mercy Ships has given him a new lease of life and in many ways these have been the best years we have ever spent together.'

Of course, not all our helpers spent long periods of time on board. Bill and Karen Hansill were on their way to the World Expo Exhibition in Vancouver, British Columbia in 1986 when they first heard about the *Anastasis*. On the ferry from Seattle to Victoria, a young exuberant couple piqued their interest with stories of the unusual hospital ship that was undergoing repairs in Victoria. They decided to investigate and, because Bill was a nurse, I was called to reception to show them around.

I looked at Bill in amazement: he was not your typical nurse, by any stretch of the imagination. His tall, lanky figure was topped by a mop of dark brown hair adorned with a bright orange streak. He laughed and talked energetically as I toured them through our scarred and dilapidated facility. Karen stood quietly by, thoughtfully absorbing all she saw.

They were not impressed with the rusty mess they inspected, yet something stirred within them. Over the previous few months they had been praying about supporting someone who was working in missions. As I showed them round, they felt God prompting them. I was to be the recipient. When a cheque arrived in the mail a couple of weeks later, I could hardly believe it. I desperately needed some extra support but had no idea how to acquire it.

Bill and Karen have supported me faithfully ever since, not just financially but in prayer as well. It has made a radical impact on their prayer life. Both of them have woken at night prompted by God to pray for me. Often he brings specific needs to their minds. On one occasion they felt God prompt them to ask if I had any unexpected demands they could help with. My sewing machine had broken down a couple of days before and they generously provided me with a new one. At another time, they were buying a new car and felt God urge them to give the old one to me. The ship's office was just in the process of moving to Texas and it was obvious I would need a vehicle to get around.

Bill has also had the opportunity to participate in several outreaches on the *Anastasis* – no longer that rusty little mess he first thought it to be. He has made two trips to Jamaica and one to Africa. Each time he was challenged afresh by the power of the gospel to heal and transform lives in both practical and spiritual ways.

Even the children of crew members make an important contribution to the ministry. Mariska Lako was only four when her parents and two-year-old sister Sandra left Holland in January 1980 to join the *Anastasis*. As an engaging pre-schooler with short blonde hair and brilliant blue eyes, she scampered round the aft deck with her friends, rapidly adopting the English language, and avidly embracing this strange new life. She quickly learned that God answers prayer and was soon praying fervently for a little baby brother. God was faithful, and a year later Stefan was born. The Lakos' lived on board until 1994 and so Mariska spent most of her childhood growing up on the *Anastasis*.

Mariska's life provided benefits few children ever realize. She had always loved singing and dancing, and on board the ship had a unique opportunity to develop this interest. In 1985 she joined a dynamic group of eight to eighteen year olds drawn from amongst the ship's children, called the Ship's Kids. Dressed in a wonderful array of costumes, from sailor suits and seaman's caps to colourful ethnic outfits, they danced around the stage, their faces glowing with their love of God and concern for others. Through creative movements and catchy songs, interspersed with short testimonies they presented the gospel story to crowds in Europe, Africa and the South Pacific. Their zeal and enthusiasm intrigued and attracted many people to God.

For Mariska, one of her most painful, yet significant memories of Ship's Kids occurred in 1992 in a village in Sierra Leone. She was now a tall elegant teenager in Senior High, and was praying seriously about her future direction. Should she be a doctor or a lawyer? It was a hard decision.

That day, Mariska's team was called to help the medical group battling a measles epidemic in the village of Makomba. She held desperately ill babies in her arms, her heart aching with the knowledge that a simple injection would have stopped all that suffering. Mariska was intimately involved with one of three children who died that day and God used that tragic incident to challenge her life. Today she is in her final year of International Baccalaureate in Holland determined to pursue a medical career. Then she wants to go back to Africa to help children who live in poverty and to share God's love with them.

Mariska told me recently, 'I haven't always loved everything about the ship. There were many times that I felt it was too small, too boring, too enclosed, too hot or too cold. Yet if I could choose a place to grow up, I couldn't have picked another place that would have provided me with what I have now – an international background, a firm foundation in the Lord, trips to all kinds of places, and a dream to heal the world. I know I can't heal the whole world, but I also know that I serve a God who can. This God can use ordinary people like me to make a difference in the physical and spiritual hunger people around me face.'

It is true: God is still actively at work in our world. Incredibly, he gives each of us the wonderful privilege of being part of that work. God endows each of us with the power to co-operate with him in healing and reconciling humanity.

The constant flow off and on the ships brought together people from a wide variety of countries and cultures. Different viewpoints and ideas ebbed and flowed in the rich multicultural mix. They challenged our own perspectives. They stretched and broadened our faith. At times they wore us to a frazzle.

I learned to appreciate that there is good and bad in every culture. I needed to affirm the good and avoid the bad. It wasn't always easy, particularly when we worked closely together.

The medical and dental teams on the *Anastasis* are always an incredibly complex multicultural mix, the ship's crew even more so. Often more than thirty nations are represented.

In the Cote d'Ivoire, we reached a peak of eighteen different nationalities in the medical department itself. Nurses, doctors, dentists and lab technicians came from Africa, North America, Western and Eastern Europe, Australia and the islands of New Zealand and the Dominican Republic. What a challenge! We were all brought up in different cultures, all speaking different languages and all trained under different medical systems. On top of that, we were all incredibly ethno-centric, that is all of us thought our way of doing things was the only right way.

Humanly speaking, I think it is impossible for such a team to work together in harmony and unity. Yet unity is essential to the accomplishment of our work and the effectiveness of our ministry. We cannot function as separate individuals if we wish to perform surgery or dentistry. Nor can we adhere rigidly to all the ways in which we were trained.

When little Wanda died on board the *Anastasis* back in the Dominican Republic, we started to appreciate the challenges of working with such a complex group. We learned some interesting lessons about ourselves and our cultures along the way.

When Wanda was first carried on board, all of us thought that we knew exactly what to do. Each of us was convinced our way was the best way to treat her. We quickly became intolerant of procedures suggested by others. As Wanda's condition deteriorated our stress levels rose and we became more and more forceful in our proclamation of the right way to do things. I wanted to give her quarter strength milk, my South African colleague was determined to use a half strength solution. A Norwegian nurse started using a rectal thermometer and her English friend angrily told her to take temperatures under the armpit. We argued about whether to weigh Wanda in kilograms or pounds. We got upset at the difference between degrees Fahrenheit and Celsius. It was all so trivial and all so difficult.

On another outreach in Jamaica, even language became a divisive issue. Of course, in order to communicate, we always had to share a common language. Everyone who came to the *Anastasis* had to speak English. However, in casual conversation a rich plethora of languages could often be heard. At times it must have sounded a little like Babel.

Under stress, people tended to revert to their native language too. On this particular outreach, the operating room team consisted of equal numbers of Dutch and English speakers. There was a constant babble of voices in two languages.

The English speakers hated being left out of a conversation, and wanted everything in English. The Dutch speakers resented being forced to communicate always in a foreign language. By the time I was called in to adjudicate, the atmosphere could be cut with a knife. It wasn't easy to reach a compromise which allowed each group the freedom to use their own languages at times. The important thing was to provide an atmosphere of acceptance and forgiveness in which each person acknowledged and accepted the differences in the others. It was only through the loving reconciling spirit of Christ that a compromise could be reached. Without Christ's loving example to guide us, I don't think any solution would have ever been possible.

I realized in the middle of these conflicts how ingrained our cultures are within us. We very easily become intolerant of those who are different, particularly when we work or live with them. God was teaching me yet another lesson. I not only needed to be more sensitive to other cultures, I also needed to actively learn more about them and appreciate their richness and diversity.

I was very proud of the fact that during my travels, I had learned to say 'Hello' in at least ten different languages. I could say 'Karle mere' in Greek, 'Bula' in Fijian and 'Guten morgen' in German. It always brought a smile to a face and a sense of unity to a situation. Embarrassingly, I never once thought to learn 'Hello' in the languages of my colleagues. Perhaps, if I had, it would have eased some of the tensions we experienced.

One of the greatest dilemmas faced by any multicultural team is recognizing the uniqueness and value of people who are very different from ourselves. Even more difficult is learning to interact in ways that respect and honour each other's individuality and culture. The challenge is to develop techniques that work together without jeopardizing the care of the patient.

I have gradually learned that all cultures are richly gifted by God. We all possess treasures, gifts and abilities to further God's Kingdom. Similarly, all of us have something to learn from those around us. Working in harmony as a team will always mean giving up a little of our own individual ways so that someone else has an opportunity to express theirs. 'In honour preferring one another,' became a real challenge when the other person's ideas were the antithesis of my own.

We cannot fully represent Christ unless we work together in unity and function as a body, particularly not in an international ministry like Mercy Ships. Seeking to understand those with whom we work, particularly those who are very different from ourselves enriches our lives and broadens our understanding of the beauty and complexity of the body which is Christ.

One scripture that has been particularly valuable to me in seeking unity and harmony with my fellow workers, is Phil 2:1–4.

> If you have any encouragement from being united with Christ, if any comfort from his love, if any fellowship with the Spirit, if any tenderness and compassion, then make my joy complete by being like-minded, having the same love, being one in spirit and purpose. Do nothing out of selfish ambition or vain conceit, but in humility consider others better than yourselves. Each of you should look not only to your own interests, but also to the interests of others.

It is such an inspiring description of the concern and care we should have for the needs of those who are working with us. If we can start with an acknowledgement of the fact that the needs of our companions are more important than our own, we would have a perfect team and maybe a perfect world.

God has created man in a wonderful kaleidoscope of personalities, cultures and creeds and in each of us he has planted a small deposit of truth about his character. To none of us has he revealed all truth, and to none of us has he given the ability to be a total reflection of all that he is. Together we form the Body of Christ, and together therefore we reflect the wonder and glory of his character.

As we grasp hold of this truth, it gives us great freedom to work with and amongst people of different cultural backgrounds. No longer are we constrained to indoctrinate them with our way of doing something, or shocked by the differences in their behaviour and practices. We are able to see reflected in their lives the image of Christ and are able to walk together with them accepting their individuality as another aspect of the complexity and wonder of God.

> Therefore as God's chosen people, holy and dearly loved, clothe yourselves with compassion, kindness, humility, gentleness, and patience. Bear with each other and forgive whatever grievances you may have against one another. Forgive as the Lord forgave you. And over all these virtues put on love, which binds them all together in perfect unity. Col 3:12–14

In the long run it is love that binds us together in an unbroken relationship – love for God and love for each other. It is this love, and not our work which will create the lasting effects for God's Kingdom. It is this love and not our own skills which speak of a God of love who cares for each individual and will make any sacrifice to draw them into relationship with himself.

One painful but very valuable lesson I learned through these cross-cultural conflicts is always to look to myself and my own shortcomings to help rectify a difficult situation. My question in the midst of conflict has come to be 'Lord, in what ways are my attitudes and shortcomings contributing to this conflict and what can I do to change that?'

When we were in Greece, a major bone of contention between myself and Doug and Kathryn Mar, was my insistence on 'the right way to make tea'. First you boil the water, then you heat the pot and then you make the tea. I shuddered at the thought of iced tea or instant tea and even hated to use tea bags.

Trivial? Maybe, yet it alienated me from my best friends. I found I had to seek their forgiveness and accept that their way too was an appropriate way to make tea. After all, the Chinese had been making tea for far longer than the Australians! I needed desperately to step outside my cultural barriers and see that my ways were not always better, they were just different.

Praying together, studying the Bible together and just having fun together, all helped build our bonds of unity. One valuable event that always seemed to assist this process was our morning devotional time. At 7.30 a.m. each morning the whole medical and dental department gathered sleepily in the forward lounge for a time of prayer and worship. Often we shared encouraging stories from the day before, or prayed about areas of conflict or need. Sometimes Dr Gary strummed his guitar and led us in a few rousing choruses, or the South Pacific Island team jerked us awake with their spirited native songs. Sometimes we shared a short scriptural devotional. By the end of our session, everyone felt refreshed and ready to face the day . . . together.

Often God's presence was tangibly in our midst during these times. He is the very necessary focus to start our day's activities. Recognizing Christ as the centre of our lives, and endeavouring to see him reflected in the faces of our co-workers, enables us to bridge the chasms that would otherwise divide and separate us irreparably.

Some of my most vivid and wonderful multicultural experiences on board the *Anastasis* revolve around the celebration of Christmas and Advent. This has always been an important season for me. Advent, looking back to Christ's birth and anticipating his coming again, always stirs my heart. Our rich multicultural celebrations on board the *Anastasis*, set in Mexico or Africa, made it even more significant.

For weeks beforehand we enthusiastically prepared for this season. A committee was formed to plan special celebrations that reflect the coming together of many different traditions from a variety of nations. We sang Christmas carols in different languages, we read the scriptures anticipating the coming of Christ and set up a manger scene in the ship's reception area. Sometimes we celebrated the associated Swedish tradition of St Lucia where young girls walked into the service, their heads aglow with a halo of lights, or St Nicholas walked the corridors on December 6th, followed by an eager crowd of Dutch children. I loved listening to the stories crew members told about Christmas in their country as they related the significance of the rich traditions that embroidered the occasion. So often this sharing helped us evaluate our own ceremonies and trappings. Why were they important? Did it really have anything to do with the coming of Christ and the true meaning of Christmas?

Christmas week there were no operations performed in the hospital and all outreach and construction teams took a well earned break. Everyone had an opportunity to participate in the joyous celebration. However, our thoughts were never far from the patients and their needs. Sometimes, one or two with lingering infections stayed with us over the Christmas season. They were enthusiastically embraced by the community and became an important part of our activities.

There were rarely Christmas lights or decorations in the surrounding villages but the ship was a joyful reflection of the season. A Christmas tree, often brown and brittle because it had been carried from Europe or the US months earlier, reached majestically up through the reception area to the landing above. It was heavily festooned with lights and rich gold and burgundy decorations. Artificial sprays of holly and fir branches twined their way up the banisters. Wreaths hung on cabin doors. Some were fashioned from local materials with splashes of rich yellow cloth and small African dolls. Others were acquired when the ship spent its first Christmas in Mexico. They were intricately woven from straw intermingled with red and green coloured yarn. Bells hung suspended in the middle. Still others reflected crew members' ethnic backgrounds. There were holly wreaths and poinsettias, Dutch clogs and Norwegian flags.

The smell of Christmas baking beckoned a temptingly welcome to passersby. Many people showed open hospitality at this season, and on one designated evening a large number of crew members opened their cabins so that visitors could go from one to another to another like a general open house.

On Christmas Eve we placed a shoe by the door of our cabins. In the morning it would be filled with a small offering – an African bracelet, or a few nuts, a scripture verse of love and blessing.

Christmas morning the ship was abuzz with

excited activity. The little children found the shoes and their treasure troves of sweets and nuts. They ran through the hot steamy corridors in nothing but their nappies, laughing and squealing their delight. Friends and families congregated early to open presents. Usually there wasn't much – none of us could afford to spend more than a few dollars on each other. Some of us had packages from home. There were mouldy brownies and chocolate chip biscuits that had sat too long in the customs shed. They were intermingled with other precious items like our favourite shampoos or a special brand of tea. We laughed and chatted together then invaded the dining room for brunch. Our usual servers had a day off, and Dr Bob stood in the serving line next to a little short guy with black shaggy hair. They cheerfully sang *Felice Navidad* to us as we accepted our scrambled eggs and bacon.

For me the highlight of the day was our Christmas service, held on the aft deck. It was a wonderful celebration of the coming of Christ into our world. We sang *Silent Night* in six different languages and I gazed around at the medley of black and brown and white worshippers. Every area of the globe was represented in the eager upturned faces and I caught a glimpse of the coming of Christ's Kingdom in which the richness of every tribe and nationality will be wonderfully manifested.

My thoughts turned to the patients who would come on board next week. The significance of Christ's sacrifice in leaving the wonders and glories of heaven to enter our world in a humble stable were heightened by our awareness of the world around. It was impossible not to be grateful that he was willing to enter our pain-racked world as a humble peasant child when we were surrounded by such suffering and need.

Finally we sat down to Christmas dinner, families and friends sharing together the joy of Christ's coming. On our first Christmas in Mexico, we wanted to make it all feel like home. Red and green streamers festooned the dining room. Candles adorned the tables. Their wax softened and sagged in the sweltering heat. When we lit them, the temperature rose dramatically and we were soon sweating uncomfortably in our Sunday best.

To me this wonderfully rich multicultural celebration of Christmas gives a little glimpse of the future of God when we will all celebrate together as an international community of God's people.

I have caught another glimpse of this as we have had unique opportunities to work together with local mission and government organizations to further their hopes and dreams for an area. Often the various practical and spiritual ministries on the *Anastasis* act as a catalyst. We have the privilege of initiating projects local people hope to establish. Our resources and labourers make possible in a few short months what might otherwise take years to accomplish. Nowhere was this better exemplified than in the ship's visit to Sierra Leone.

When the *Anastasis* assessment teams arrived a year before the ship's visit to Sierra Leone, they were introduced to the Bread of Life Project. This collaborative group was begun by Scripture Union and the Fellowship of Evangelical Students (SUFES). It developed an impressive five-year strategy to provide some 10,000 villagers with preventative health care, training, employment and opportunities for income generation. Their efforts centred around the village of Makomba, which so radically changed Mariska Lako's life. This poor, predominantly Muslim community lies 30 miles south-east of Freetown, along a deeply rutted dirt road. Their programme, with its ministries of mercy combined with evangelism, paralleled that of Mercy Ships and we soon eagerly developed a partnership.

To generate income, workers in the village began an extensive garden on the 40-acre site. Tall palm oil trees soon waved their proud heads above the fields. Rich green cassava, potatoes and other vegetables sprouted from the soil providing an abundant harvest to sell in the local market.

When the *Anastasis* arrived, the work progressed rapidly. Our relief and development team, laboured side by side with the SUFES people to build a multi-purpose concrete storage building. They also installed an irrigation and rain harvesting system, planted a pineapple crop and developed model gardens. They fenced the property and excavated a pond for fresh water. Mercy Ships provided tools, seed, fertilizer, labourers and training.

Then the *Anastasis* medical team came to the area. They arrived at the height of a devastating measles epidemic and were inundated with sick and often dehydrated children. An outdoor hospital ward blossomed on the straw ground under a thatched roof. The doctors and nurses inserted nasogastric tubes and administered IV fluids fighting valiantly to save children's lives. Some they couldn't save. The tiny bodies were already too drained by malnutrition and disease. Others responded well, and soon scampered gleefully around the ward with renewed energy.

Evangelism teams came to help. They comforted anxious crying mothers and grandmothers. They controlled the crowds, comforted them and prayed with them. They performed dramas and shared evangelistic messages, challenging the crowds with stories of a God who cared for all their needs, physical, emotional and spiritual. By the time the ship left Sierra Leone, the young eager SUFES workers were already holding Bible studies in the new facility and their students were sharing the gospel on a regular basis with the people of Makomba.

Much to our delight, 16 eager students from 8 surrounding villages participated in a community health education programme. They proudly graduated with certificates showing completion of the course. It is exciting to think that the work we began will go on under the auspices of this local group. The establishment of an immunization programme will hopefully prevent the recurrence of the tragic measles epidemic which claimed several lives. The nutritional training and market gardening will have a long-term impact on eradication of malnutrition.

It is exhilarating and challenging to see how God works. He brings together people from so many different places and with many different backgrounds at the right time to accomplish his purposes. To work in partnership with people from many parts of the world is a rich and rewarding aspect of any overseas ministry.

To have people from so many different nations working together in harmony is no small feat. It is a wonderful testimony to the grace of God who created humankind in the beautiful array of cultures, creeds and tribes we see around us. Above all it should be both a remembrance of that first Pentecost, and a foretaste of the wonderful richness and complexity of the new community of Christ which brings together men and women from every background, culture and creed to become a part of God's new humanity.

Chapter 14

A FINAL WORD

'I think what you do is so wonderful,' said the starry eyed young woman who bounced up to me after I spoke at a recent conference. 'Unfortunately I couldn't do what you're doing,' she continued with a sigh of relief. 'I get seasick.'

Thinking to reassure her, I shared my own encounters with seasickness. I vividly related how I had managed through these difficult episodes. She became more and more uncomfortable. She began to squirm and her face reflected a spark of fear. By the time I finished talking she was ready to run away from me. Suddenly it hit me. 'She doesn't really want to know how she can get involved in Christian work. All she wants is an excuse for her own comfortable way of life. What a shame she doesn't realize what she is missing out on.'

As I watched the woman's rapidly retreating form, my thoughts raced back over the years. I remembered my own reservations back in New Zealand in the late 70s. My life too had been very comfortable, ensconced in my family practice and beautiful Christchurch home. In those days, I understood faith in very private terms that fully sanctioned my self-centred way of life. Sadly, this way of life had virtually no room for the poor or even for the other members of Christ's international body in other lands.

When we started this journey, together in Greece in 1981, the *Anastasis* – the Resurrection – was in the graveyard. I was an eager young missionary doctor ready to change the world. What I wasn't prepared for was my own graveyard experiences and the major renovation process God planned on my life.

In Greece, in Thailand, in Central America and Africa, God scraped and chipped away at the layers of paint, the rust and the dirt that constituted my grave clothes. God overhauled my life and resurrected it as dramatically as he did the *Anastasis*. God began by broadening my theology, opening my heart in new ways and fundamentally changing my values and my lifestyle.

First, through the international community within Mercy Ships, my view of the faithfulness of God expanded. In Greece, as I was forced to depend on others for financial support, encouragement and direction I realized how interdependent we all are. Each of us needs the help of the other members of the community of God in order to become all God intends for us to be. Through these experiences, I learned to pray and depend on God in a way I never had to do when I earned a predictable income.

Through working in Thailand, Africa, the Caribbean and other developing nations, my view of the world and the people we share it with was also dramatically changed. In these new and often challenging environments I became aware that it is not just our friends and immediate community who contribute to our faith and view of God. The poverty-stricken and destitute of the world have much to teach us about our caring, compassionate God who cares desperately for their plight. My sisters and brothers from Africa, South America and Asia have taught me valuable lessons I would never have learned working in any Western nation, even my own. As I held dying children in my arms, I knew God grieved far more than I did for their suffering. As I rejoiced with a mother whose malnourished child had just taken its first meal and stepped away from the precipice of death, I sensed God rejoiced with me.

That's why my time in Thailand was so shattering. Suddenly, I was thrust into a situation in which I was surrounded by unbelievable human suffering. Dying children for whom I could do nothing left me feeling helpless and inadequate. More to the point, there was absolutely no place in my very private Christian faith for the agony I encountered and I quickly realized God had a very big place in his heart for these people. It was time for me to go back to school again, scrape away a little more rust, and develop a faith and theology that was as broad as the heart of God.

It was then that I came across Ron Sider's book *Rich Christians in an Age of Hunger*. It dramatically challenged my life and began to expand my faith. As Ron Sider affirms: 'God not only acts in history to liberate the poor, but in a mysterious way that we can only half fathom, the Sovereign of the universe identifies with the weak and the destitute'[5]. Not only does God identify with the poor, but it occurred to me that he expects us to, as well.

God used many new experiences to shake up my life and in so doing, helped me discover a much broader sense of purpose for my existence. Much to my amazement, I discovered I enjoyed working with my friends from all over the world far more than I ever had in my self-involved life in New Zealand. God not only chipped off the rough edges, he remodelled my interior life as well.

In my travels, as I watched the very different ways people from other cultures related to God, I realized too how inadequate my view of him was. Lesslie Newbigin expresses this so aptly in his important book *Foolishness To The Greeks*[6]: 'The fact that Jesus is much more than, much greater than our culture-bound vision of him can only come home to us through the witness of those who see him with other eyes.' I learned to see Jesus through African eyes, Tongan eyes and Cambodian eyes. Now the Jesus that I follow has far more form and substance than the culturally bound Jesus of my early Christian life.

Most challenging of all were the expressions of spirituality in primal African cultures. For these people, religion embraced all areas of their lives. It was present in the created world and the spirits of water, earth, sun and moon. It was essential to the understanding of health and disease. The balance between life and death was often perceived as depending on the development of good relationships, right behaviour and appeasement of spirits as well as the more practical aspects of nutrition and germs.

As I observed these people living in a world in which their spiritual practices impinged on every aspect of life, I could not but help comparing it to my Western Christianity. 'Is Christianity intended to be as all-embracing as their religions?' I pondered. 'Or is it really only concerned with a compartmentalized, personal salvation and transformation of body, soul and spirit? Is Christianity too, supposed to impinge on the whole of life and affect every aspect of creation?' and more importantly, 'How does this affect the way I practise my Christianity and live my own life?'

As I struggled through this season of learning, I believe I emerged with a more complete biblical understanding of my Christian faith. Building on the foundations developed in Greece and Thailand, the challenges of African culture helped me realize my need for a view of Christian faith that was far more inclusive than my own personal redemption. God's love embraces the whole of our world and every creature he has created. He not only wanted to change my heart, and the way I lived my life. God wanted to transform a world.

The more I travelled and studied, the more I was convinced that all Christians require a vision that encompasses every aspect of life. I learned from scripture that God wants to change our aspirations, our vocations and our life direction to focus on his all-embracing vision, not our personal agendas. I learned that every part of the way we live needs to be consistent with the purposes of God in our world.

This broadening understanding brought me back to those verses from Isaiah 35 that God impressed on us during our early development of the ship's medical ministry.

Then will the eyes of the blind be opened and the ears of the deaf unstopped. Then will the lame leap like a deer, and the mute tongue shout for joy. Water will gush forth in the wilderness and streams in the desert. The burning sand will become a pool, the thirsty ground bubbling springs.

Now as my vision of God's purposes broadened, these verses took on new meaning. I suddenly realized that they offered far more than encouragement for a struggling missionary. These verses expressed a wonderful promise from God, a promise that went far beyond the ministry that I was involved in. These verses reflect a view of God's future in which all things are made new. It is a view of the future expounded in even more wonderful terms in Isaiah 25:6–9

> On this mountain the Lord Almighty will prepare a feast of rich food for all peoples, a banquet of aged wine – the best of meats and the finest of wines. On this mountain he will destroy the shroud that enfolds all peoples, the sheet that covers all nations; he will swallow up death for ever. The Sovereign Lord will wipe away the tears from all faces; he will remove the disgrace of his people from all the earth. The Lord has spoken.

I believe this is the vision of the future toward which God calls us, whether we travel abroad or stay at home. It is a view of Christianity that encompasses all of humanity – our families, our churches, our communities – and also our world and the whole of God's beautiful creation. It is a view of the future that is filled with hope and celebration rather than pain and despair. When one anticipates the restoration of all things in Christ not just in our own personal lives, or in relationship with others, but in all peoples and cultures, not only do we have hope, we have new reason for life itself.

Walter Bruggemann helped make this concept come to life for me in his exciting book *Living Toward a Vision: Biblical Reflections on Shalom*. 'He identified the biblical term that best describes this vision of one community embracing all of creation, as the word 'shalom'. To the Hebrews 'shalom' was more than just a word of greeting or a sense of personal peace. It carried with it a promise of hope for the future and the anticipation of a time in which justice would come for the poor, freedom for the oppressed, healing for the lame and the sick and restoration of all creation.

Shalom in all its power is well-being that exists in the very midst of threats – from sword and drought, and from wild animals. It is well-being of a material, physical, historical kind, not idyllic 'pie in the sky', but 'salvation' in the midst of trees and crops and enemies – in the very places where people always have to cope with anxiety, struggle for survival, and deal with temptation. It is well-being of a very personal kind, but it is also deliberately corporate. If there is to be well-being, it will not be just for isolated, insulated individuals; it is rather security and prosperity granted to a whole community – young and old, rich and poor, powerful and dependent. Always we are all in it together. Together we stand before God's blessings and together we receive the gift of life if we receive it at all. Shalom comes only to the inclusive, embracing community that excludes none.

The vision of wholeness, which is the supreme will of the Biblical God, is the outgrowth of 'shalom' (Ez 34:25), in which persons are bound not only to God but to one another in a caring sharing rejoicing community with none to make them afraid.

I love this vision of 'shalom' that God called me to on this journey. It offers us a new way of relating that binds us together in a wonderful caring, loving relationship to our sisters and brothers in all Christian community throughout the world. More powerfully still, it reminds us of our connection to the earth itself and our need for proper stewardship of God's wonderful creation. Finally, it reminds me of how deeply our God loves us and longs to redeem us. He wants to make us members of the international family of God.

The early church, as shown in the book of Acts, truly knew what 'shalom' was all about. For the early Christians, faith embraced and radically transformed the whole of life. Their lives focused on healing the sick, feeding the hungry and caring for the dispossessed. They offered a loving, caring community in which to dwell. They were not only concerned about every aspect of a person's individual life, but also with the needs of the community and the world around.

Most wonderfully of all, this vision of 'shalom' points us towards Christ, in whom all persons and all things will be restored. 'He is our peace' – our 'shalom'. Christ Jesus is the one who guides us towards that vision of a better future so wonderfully anticipated throughout Isaiah, and so beautifully summarized in Revelation 21:1–4.

> Then I saw a new heaven and a new earth, for the first heaven and the first earth had passed away, and there was no longer any sea. I saw the Holy City, the new Jerusalem, coming down out of heaven from God, prepared as a bride beautifully dressed for her husband. And I heard a loud voice from the throne saying, 'Now the dwelling of God is with men and he will live with them. They will be his people, and God himself will be with them and be their God. He will wipe every tear from their eyes. There will be no more death or mourning or crying or pain, for the old order of things has passed away.'

As we accept this compelling vision for our lives,

we cannot help but be changed. Each time we heal the sick, feed the hungry and preach good news to the poor, we catch a glimpse of God's kingdom and experience a little of his 'shalom' vision for the world. I have seen it so vividly in the images of life on board the *Anastasis*. Each time we expressed concern for each other by sharing finances and encouragement, each time we helped a person see or transformed their faces, each time we evangelized and shared the love of God, we saw a little of God's Kingdom in our midst.

So it is for all our lives. As we look to the future God challenges us to participate in bringing his Kingdom into being. Through our actions, and the outpouring of our faith – in love, in relationship and in caring – we can all live in the 'shalom' future of God, today.

I hope you have enjoyed this odyssey with a seasick doctor. I hope some of what I have experienced in the good times and the hard times has made something of God's 'shalom' and love real to you. I would urge you to try what I tried back in 1981. Step out and take a risk. God might not be calling you to sign up on the *Anastasis*, but maybe there are some at risk kids or neglected seniors in your community who need to know something of the 'shalom' love of God. I would encourage you to try and put God's purposes first in your life. I suspect if you do, you will discover as I did, that the life given away is much more satisfying than life kept to ourselves.

'Through compassionate action, the old is not just old anymore and pain is not just pain any longer. Although we are still waiting in expectation, the first signs of the new earth and the new heaven, which have been promised to us and for which we hope, are already visible in the community of faith where the compassionate God reveals Himself. This is the foundation of our faith, the basis of our hope and the source of our love'[8].

NOTES

1. *Rich Christians in an Age of Hunger* Ronald J. Sider; InterVarsity Press, Downers Grove, Il 60515; 1977

2. *Healing* Francis MacNutt; o.p. Ave Maria Press, Notre Dame Indiana; 1974

3. *Health, Healing and Transformation* E. Anthony Allen, Kenneth L. Luscombe, Bryant L. Myers, Eric R. Ram; MARC/World Vision International, Monrovia, California; 1991

4. *Health, Healing and Transformation* p 60

5. *Rich Christians in an Age of Hunger* p 68, Ron Sider; IVP; 1977

6. *Foolishness to the Greeks: The Gospel and Western Culture* p 146, Lesslie Newbigin; Wm B Eerdman, Grand Rapids Mich 49503; 1986

7. *Living Toward a Vision: Biblical Reflections on Shalom* p 16, Walter Bruggemann; United Church Press New York

8. *Compassion – A Reflection on the Christian Life* p 135, Henri J.M. Nouwen, Donald P. McNeill, Douglas A. Morrison; Image Books Doubleday, New York; 1983